MW00560133

CONTENTS

INTRODUCTION

Do you want a smart multipurpose oven that could bake, roast, and air fry? Or do you like to upgrade your kitchen with a space-friendly cooking appliance? Then look no further, as the Ninja Foodi Digital Air Fryer Oven offers you all in one place. The Air fryer oven technology is not new, but Ninja Foodi has managed to bring innovation by launching this 8 in 1 multifunctional digital oven. There are several distinctive features of this oven that will leave you awestruck and even toasting and roasting being on top of all. And if you want to try all of its smart cooking functions, then this book comes as a right read for you. It has all the delicious recipes that you can bake and cook in this appliance. Whether it's the crispy Air fried snacks or baked morning bread, roast meat, or toasted bagels, you can cook it all with your Ninja digital oven.

And once you are done cooking, you can pull the appliance and make it stan in a vertical position to create lots of space on your kitchen counter. This is the reason that this digital oven stands apart from similar ovens in the market; despite its XL size, managing counter space is not a problem when you buy Ninja foodi air fryer oven. This oven fits perfectly in the kitchen of all sizes. Now you can cook large portion sizes in a single session using this appliance.

Smart Cooking Programs:

The Ninja Foodi Digital Air fryer oven offers eight different cooking modes. It's a powerful heating system that runs on 1800, watt cooks food evenly and in a short time. The oven has the following cooking modes:

- Air Fry
- Air Roast
- Air Broil
- Bake
- Dehydrate
- Keep Warm
- Toast
- Bagel

After selecting the desired cooking mode, the cooking time and temperature can be selected using the rotating dial. The appliance automatically preheats once given instructions. For toasting, the user can select the number of slices and the level of darkness as well.

BREAKFAST AND BRUNCH RECIPES

Sweet Potato Tots

Servings: 4
Cooking Time: 1 Hour

Ingredients:

- 1 tablespoon of potato starch
- 2 small sweet potatoes, peeled
- 1-1/4 teaspoons kosher salt
- 1/8 teaspoon of garlic powder
- ¾ cup ketchup

Directions:

1. Boil water in a medium-sized pot over high heat.
2. Add the potatoes. Cook till it becomes tender. Transfer them to a plate for cooling. Grate them in a mid-sized bowl.
3. Toss gently with garlic powder, 1 teaspoon of salt, and potato starch.
4. Shape the mix into tot-shaped cylinders.
5. Apply cooking spray on the air fryer basket.
6. Place half of the tots in a later in your basket. Apply some cooking spray.
7. Cook till it becomes light brown at 400°F.
8. Take out from the frying basket. Sprinkle some salt.
9. Serve with ketchup immediately.

Nutrition Info: Calories 80, Carbohydrates 19g, Total Fat 0g, Protein 1g, Fiber 2g, Sodium 335mg, Sugars 8g

Cinnamon French Toasts

Servings: 2
Cooking Time: 5 Minutes

Ingredients:

- 2 eggs
- ¼ cup whole milk
- 3 tablespoons sugar
- 2 teaspoons olive oil
- 1/8 teaspoon vanilla extract
- 1/8 teaspoon ground cinnamon
- 4 bread slices

Directions:

1. In a large bowl, add all the ingredients except for bread slices and mix well.
2. Coat the bread slices with egg mixture evenly.
3. Press "Power Button" of Ninja Foodi Digital Air Fry Oven and turn the dial to select "Air Fry" mode.
4. Press "Time Button" and again turn the dial to set the cooking time to 6 minutes.
5. Now push "Temp Button" and rotate the dial to set the temperature at 390 degrees F.
6. Press "Start/Pause" button to start.
7. When the unit beeps to show that it is preheated, open the lid and lightly grease the sheet pan.
8. Arrange the bread slices into the air fry basket and insert in the oven.
9. Flip the bread slices once halfway through.
10. When cooking time is complete, open the lid and transfer the French toast onto serving plates.
11. Serve warm.
12. Serving Suggestions: You can enjoy these French toast with the drizzling of maple syrup.
13. Variation Tip: For best result, soak the bread slices in egg mixture until each slice is thoroughly saturated.

Nutrition Info: Calories: 238 Fat: 10.6g Sat Fat: 2.7g Carbohydrates: 20.8g Fiber: 0.5g Sugar: 0.9g Protein: 7.9g

French Toast Sticks

Servings: 2
Cooking Time: 10 Minutes

Ingredients:

- 4 slices of thick bread
- 2 eggs, lightly beaten
- 1 teaspoon cinnamon
- 1 teaspoon of vanilla extract
- ¼ cup milk

Directions:

1. Cut the bread into slices for making sticks.
2. Keep parchment paper on the air fryer basket's bottom.
3. Preheat your air fryer to 180 degrees C or 360 degrees F.
4. Now stir together the milk, eggs, cinnamon, vanilla extract, and nutmeg (optional). Combine well.
5. Dip each bread piece into the egg mix. Submerge well.
6. Remove the excess fluid by shaking it well.
7. Keep them in the fryer basket in a single layer.
8. Cook without overcrowding your fryer.

Nutrition Info: Calories 241, Carbohydrates 29g, Cholesterol 188mg, Total Fat 9g, Protein 11g, Fiber 2g, Sodium 423mg, Sugars 4g

Tex-mex Hash Browns

Servings: 4
Cooking Time: 30 Minutes

Ingredients:

- 1-1/2 24 oz. potatoes, cut and peeled
- 1 onion, cut into small pieces
- 1 tablespoon of olive oil
- 1 jalapeno, seeded and cut
- 1 red bell pepper, seeded and cut

Directions:

1. Soak the potatoes in water.
2. Preheat your air fryer to 160 degrees C or 320 degrees F.
3. Drain and dry the potatoes using a clean towel.
4. Keep in a bowl.
5. Drizzle some olive oil over the potatoes, coat well.
6. Transfer to the air frying basket.
7. Add the onion, jalapeno, and bell pepper in the bowl.
8. Sprinkle half teaspoon olive oil, pepper, and salt. Coat well by tossing.
9. Now transfer your potatoes to the bowl with the veg mix from your fryer.
10. Place the empty basket into the air fryer. Raise the temperature to 180 degrees C or 356 degrees F.
11. Toss the contents of your bowl for mixing the potatoes with the vegetables evenly.
12. Transfer mix into the basket.
13. Cook until the potatoes have become crispy and brown.

Nutrition Info: Calories 197, Carbohydrates 34g, Cholesterol 0mg, Total Fat 5g, Protein 4g, Fiber 5g, Sodium 79mg, Sugars 3g

Spinach & Tomato Frittata

Servings: 6
Cooking Time: 30 Minutes
Ingredients:
- 10 large eggs
- Salt and freshly ground black pepper, to taste
- 1 (5-ounce) bag baby spinach
- 2 cups grape tomatoes, halved
- 4 scallions, sliced thinly
- 8 ounces feta cheese, crumbled
- 3 tablespoons hot olive oil

Directions:
1. In a bowl, place the eggs, salt and black pepper and beat well.
2. Add the spinach, tomatoes, scallions and feta cheese and gently stir to combine.
3. Spread the oil in a baking pan and top with the spinach mixture.
4. Press "Power Button" of Ninja Foodi Digital Air Fry Oven and turn the dial to select "Air Bake" mode.
5. Press "Time Button" and again turn the dial to set the cooking time to 30 minutes.
6. Now push "Temp Button" and rotate the dial to set the temperature at 350 degrees F.
7. Press "Start/Pause" button to start.
8. When the unit beeps to show that it is preheated, open the lid.
9. Arrange pan over the wire rack and insert in the oven.
10. When cooking time is complete, open the lid and place the pan aside for about 5 minutes.
11. Cut into equal-sized wedges and serve hot.
12. Serving Suggestions: Enjoy your frittata with garlicky potatoes.
13. Variation Tip: Pick the right cheese for frittata.

Nutrition Info: Calories: 298 Fat: 23.6g Sat Fat: 9.3g Carbohydrates: 6.1g Fiber: 1.5g Sugar: 4.1g Protein: 17.2g

Breakfast Frittata

Servings: 2

Cooking Time: 20 Minutes

Ingredients:

- 4 eggs, beaten lightly
- 4 oz. sausages, cooked and crumbled
- 1 onion, chopped
- 2 tablespoons of red bell pepper, diced
- ½ cup shredded Cheddar cheese

Directions:

1. Bring together the cheese, eggs, sausage, onion, and bell pepper in a bowl.
2. Mix well.
3. Preheat your air fryer to 180 degrees C or 360 degrees F.
4. Apply cooking spray lightly.
5. Keep your egg mix in a prepared cake pan.
6. Now cook in your air fryer till the frittata has become set.

Nutrition Info: Calories 487, Carbohydrates 3g, Cholesterol 443mg, Total Fat 39g, Protein 31g, Fiber 0.4g, Sodium 694mg, Sugars 1g

Egg & Potato Hash

Servings: 1
Cooking Time: 20 Minutes
Ingredients:
- 2 bacon slices, halved
- 2 small potatoes, chopped
- ¼ of tomato, chopped
- 1 egg
- 2 tablespoons cheddar cheese, shredded

Directions:
1. Arrange the bacon strips onto a double layer of tin foil.
2. Place the potatoes and tomato n top of the bacon.
3. Carefully crack the egg on top of the veggie mixture.
4. With the tin foil, shape the mixture into a bowl.
5. Press "Power Button" of Ninja Foodi Digital Air Fry Oven and turn the dial to select "Air Roast" mode.
6. Press "Time Button" and again turn the dial to set the cooking time to 20 minutes.
7. Now push "Temp Button" and rotate the dial to set the temperature at 350 degrees F.
8. Press "Start/Pause" button to start.
9. When the unit beeps to show that it is preheated, open the lid.
10. Carefully arrange the foil piece over the wire rack and insert in the oven.
11. After 16 minutes of cooking, top the hash with cheese.
12. When cooking time is complete, open the lid and transfer the foil pieces onto serving plates.
13. Serve hot.
14. Serving Suggestions: Garnishing of fresh parsley will enhance the taste of this potato hash.
15. Variation Tip: Use the right kind of potatoes.

Nutrition Info: Calories: 326 Fat: 13.4g Sat Fat: 5.9g Carbohydrates: 36.8g Fiber: 5.6g Sugar: 3.4g Protein: 15.9g

Tomato Quiche

Servings: 2
Cooking Time: 30 Minutes
Ingredients:

- 4 eggs
- ¼ cup onion, chopped
- ½ cup tomatoes, chopped
- ½ cup milk
- 1 cup Gouda cheese, shredded
- Salt, to taste

Directions:

1. In a small baking pan, add all the ingredients and mix well.
2. Press "Power Button" of Ninja Foodi Digital Air Fry Oven and turn the dial to select "Air Fry" mode.
3. Press "Time Button" and again turn the dial to set the cooking time to 30 minutes.
4. Now push "Temp Button" and rotate the dial to set the temperature at 340 degrees F.
5. Press "Start/Pause" button to start.
6. When the unit beeps to show that it is preheated, open the lid.
7. Arrange the pan over the wire rack and insert in the oven.
8. When cooking time is complete, open the lid and place the pan aside for about 5 minutes.
9. Cut into equal-sized wedges and serve.
10. Serving Suggestions: Fresh baby spring mix will be a great companion for this quiche.
11. Variation Tip: You can use any kind of fresh veggies for the filling of quiche.

Nutrition Info: Calories: 247 Fat: 16.1g Sat Fat: 7.5g Carbohydrates: 7.3g Fiber: 0.9g Sugar: 5.2g Protein: 18.6g

Eggs With Chicken

Servings: 3
Cooking Time: 12 Minutes
Ingredients:
- 4 large eggs, divided
- 2 tablespoons heavy cream
- Salt and ground black pepper, as required
- 2 teaspoons unsalted butter, softened
- 2 ounces cooked chicken, chopped
- 3 tablespoons Parmesan cheese, grated finely
- 2 teaspoons fresh parsley, minced

Directions:
1. In a bowl, add 1 egg, cream, salt and black pepper and beat until smooth.
2. In the bottom of a pie pan, place the butter and spread evenly.
3. In the bottom of pie pan, place chicken over butter and top with the egg mixture evenly.
4. Carefully, crack the remaining eggs on top.
5. Sprinkle with salt and black pepper and top with cheese and parsley evenly.
6. Press "Power Button" of Ninja Foodi Digital Air Fry Oven and turn the dial to select the "Air Fry" mode.
7. Press the Time button and again turn the dial to set the cooking time to 12 minutes.
8. Now push the Temp button and rotate the dial to set the temperature at 320 degrees F.
9. Press "Start/Pause" button to start.
10. When the unit beeps to show that it is preheated, open the lid.
11. Arrange pan over the "Wire Rack" and insert in the oven.
12. Cut into equal-sized wedges and serve hot.
13. Serve hot.

Nutrition Info: Calories 199 Total Fat 14.7 g Saturated Fat 6.7 g Cholesterol 287 mg Sodium 221 mg Total Carbs 0.8 g Fiber 0 g Sugar 0.5 g Protein 16.1 g

Baked Eggs

Servings: 4
Cooking Time: 12 Minutes

Ingredients:

- 1 cup marinara sauce, divided
- 1 tablespoon capers, drained and divided
- 8 eggs
- ¼ cup whipping cream, divided
- ¼ cup Parmesan cheese, shredded and divided
- Salt and ground black pepper, as required

Directions:

1. Grease 4 ramekins. Set aside.
2. Divide the marinara sauce in the bottom of each prepared ramekin evenly and top with capers.
3. Carefully, crack 2 eggs over marinara sauce into each ramekin and top with cream, followed by the Parmesan cheese.
4. Sprinkle each ramekin with salt and black pepper.
5. Press "Power Button" of Ninja Foodi Digital Air Fry Oven and turn the dial to select the "Air Bake" mode.
6. Press the Time button and again turn the dial to set the cooking time to 12 minutes.
7. Now push the Temp button and rotate the dial to set the temperature at 400 degrees F.
8. Press "Start/Pause" button to start.
9. When the unit beeps to show that it is preheated, open the lid.
10. Arrange the ramekins over the "Wire Rack" and insert in the oven.
11. Serve warm.

Nutrition Info: Calories 223 Total Fat 14.1 g Saturated Fat 5.5 g Cholesterol 341 mg Sodium 569 mg Total Carbs 9.8 g Fiber 1.7 g Sugar 6.2 g Protein 14.3 g

Chicken & Zucchini Omelet

Servings: 6
Cooking Time: 35 Minutes

Ingredients:

- 8 eggs
- ½ cup milk
- Salt and freshly ground black pepper, to taste
- 1 cup cooked chicken, chopped
- 1 cup Cheddar cheese, shredded
- ½ cup fresh chives, chopped
- ¾ cup zucchini, chopped

Directions:

1. In a bowl, add the eggs, milk, salt and black pepper and beat well.
2. Add the remaining ingredients and stir to combine.
3. Place the mixture into a greased baking pan.
4. Press "Power Button" of Ninja Foodi Digital Air Fry Oven and turn the dial to select "Air Bake" mode.
5. Press "Time Button" and again turn the dial to set the cooking time to 35 minutes.
6. Now push "Temp Button" and rotate the dial to set the temperature at 315 degrees F.
7. Press "Start/Pause" button to start.
8. When the unit beeps to show that it is preheated, open the lid.
9. Arrange pan over the wire rack and insert in the oven.
10. When cooking time is complete, open the lid and place the baking pan aside for about 5 minutes.
11. Cut into equal-sized wedges and serve hot.
12. Serving Suggestions: Toasted bread slices will go great with this omelet.
13. Variation Tip: You can stuff this omelet with any cooked meat like turkey, bacon, crab oe sausage.

Nutrition Info: Calories: 209 Fat: 13.3g Sat Fat: 6.3g Carbohydrates: 2.3g Fiber: 0.3g Sugar: 1.8g Protein: 9.8g

Eggs In Bread Cups

Servings: 4
Cooking Time: 23 Minutes

Ingredients:
- 4 bacon slices
- 2 bread slices, crust removed
- 4 eggs
- Salt and freshly ground black pepper, to taste

Directions:
1. Grease 4 cups of a muffin tin and set aside.
2. Heat a small frying pan over medium-high heat and cook the bacon slices for about 2-3 minutes.
3. With a slotted spoon, transfer the bacon slice onto a paper towel-lined plate to cool.
4. Break each bread slice in half.
5. Arrange 1 bread slices half in each of the prepared muffin cup and press slightly.
6. Now, arrange 1 bacon slice over each bread slice in a circular shape.
7. Crack 1 egg into each muffin cup and sprinkle with salt and black pepper.
8. Press "Power Button" of Ninja Foodi Digital Air Fry Oven and turn the dial to select "Air Bake" mode.
9. Press "Time Button" and again turn the dial to set the cooking time to 20 minutes.
10. Now push "Temp Button" and rotate the dial to set the temperature at 350 degrees F.
11. Press "Start/Pause" button to start.
12. When the unit beeps to show that it is preheated, open the lid.
13. Arrange the muffin tin over the wire rack and insert in the oven.
14. When cooking time is complete, open the lid and place the muffin tin onto a wire rack for about 10 minutes.
15. Serve warm.
16. Serving Suggestions: Feel free to top the bread cups with fresh herbs of your choice before serving.
17. Variation Tip: Pancetta can be used instead of bacon.

Nutrition Info: Calories: 98 Fat: 6.6g Sat Fat: 2.1g Carbohydrates: 2.6g Fiber: 0.1g Sugar: 0.5g Protein: 7.3g

Banana Bread

Servings: 8
Cooking Time: 45 Minutes

Ingredients:

- ¾ cup whole wheat flour
- 2 medium ripe mashed bananas
- 2 large eggs
- 1 teaspoon of Vanilla extract
- ¼ teaspoon Baking soda
- ½ cup granulated sugar

Directions:

1. Keep parchment paper at the bottom of your pan. Apply some cooking spray.
2. Whisk together the baking soda, salt, flour, and cinnamon (optional) in a bowl.
3. Keep it aside.
4. Take another bowl and bring together the eggs, bananas, vanilla, and yogurt (optional) in it.
5. Stir the wet ingredients gently into your flour mix. Combine well.
6. Now pour your batter into the pan. You can also sprinkle some walnuts.
7. Heat your air fryer to 310°F. Cook till it turns brown.
8. Keep the bread on your wire rack so that it cools in the pan. Slice.

Nutrition Info: Calories 240, Carbohydrates 29g, Total Fat 12g, Protein 4g, Fiber 2g, Sodium 184mg, Sugars 17g

Bacon & Spinach Muffins

Servings: 6
Cooking Time: 17 Minutes

Ingredients:

- 6 eggs
- ½ cup milk
- Salt and freshly ground black pepper, to taste
- 1 cup fresh spinach, chopped
- 4 cooked bacon slices, crumbled

Directions:

1. In a bowl, add the eggs, milk, salt and black pepper and beat until well combined.
2. Add the spinach and stir to combine.
3. Divide the spinach mixture into 6 greased cups of an egg bite mold evenly.
4. Press "Power Button" of Ninja Foodi Digital Air Fry Oven and turn the dial to select "Air Fry" mode.
5. Press "Time Button" and again turn the dial to set the cooking time to 17 minutes.
6. Now push "Temp Button" and rotate the dial to set the temperature at 325 degrees F.
7. Press "Start/Pause" button to start.
8. When the unit beeps to show that it is preheated, open the lid.
9. Arrange the mold over the wire rack and insert in the oven.
10. When cooking time is complete, open the lid and place the mold onto a wire rack to cool for about 5 minutes.
11. Top with bacon pieces and serve warm.
12. Serving Suggestions: Serve these muffins with the drizzling of melted butter.
13. Variation Tip: Don't forget to grease the egg bite molds before pacing the egg mixture in them.

Nutrition Info: Calories: 179 Fat: 12.9g Sat Fat: 4.3g Carbohydrates: 1.8g Fiber: 0.1g Sugar: 1.3g Protein: 13.5g

Potato Rosti

Servings: 2
Cooking Time: 15 Minutes
Ingredients:

- ½ pound potatoes, peeled, grated and squeezed
- ½ tablespoon fresh rosemary, chopped finely
- ½ tablespoon fresh thyme, chopped finely
- 1/8 teaspoon red pepper flakes, crushed
- Salt and ground black pepper, as required
- 2 tablespoons butter, softened

Directions:
1. In a bowl, mix together the potato, herbs, red pepper flakes, salt and black pepper.
2. Press "Power Button" of Ninja Foodi Digital Air Fry Oven and turn the dial to select the "Air Fry" mode.
3. Press the Time button and again turn the dial to set the cooking time to 15 minutes.
4. Now push the Temp button and rotate the dial to set the temperature at 355 degrees F.
5. Press "Start/Pause" button to start.
6. When the unit beeps to show that it is preheated, open the lid and lightly, grease the sheet pan.
7. Arrange the potato mixture into the "Sheet Pan" and shape it into an even circle.
8. Insert the "Sheet Pan" in the oven.
9. Cut the potato rosti into wedges.
10. Top with the butter and serve immediately.

Nutrition Info: Calories 185 Total Fat 11.8 g Saturated Fat 7.4 g Cholesterol 31 mg Sodium 167 mg Total Carbs 18.9 g Fiber 3.4 g Sugar 1.3 g Protein 2.1 g

Loaded Potatoes

Servings: 2
Cooking Time: 15 Minutes
Ingredients:

- 11 oz. baby potatoes
- 2 cut bacon slices
- 1-1/2 oz. low-fat cheddar cheese, shredded
- 1 teaspoon of olive oil
- 2 tablespoons low-fat sour cream

Directions:
1. Toss the potatoes with oil.
2. Place them in your air fryer basket. Cook till they get tender at 350°F. stir occasionally.
3. Cook the bacon meanwhile in a skillet till it gets crispy.
4. Take out the bacon from your pan. Crumble.
5. Keep the potatoes on a serving plate. Crush them lightly to split.
6. Top with cheese, chives, salt, crumbled bacon, and sour cream.

Nutrition Info: Calories 240, Carbohydrates 26g, Total Fat 12g, Protein 7g, Fiber 4g, Sodium 287mg, Sugars 3g

Cheese Toasts With Eggs & Bacon

Servings: 2
Cooking Time: 4 Minutes
Ingredients:

- 4 bread slices
- 1 garlic clove, minced
- 4 ounces goat cheese, crumbled
- Freshly ground black pepper, to taste
- 2 hard-boiled eggs, peeled and chopped
- 4 cooked bacon slices, crumbled

Directions:

1. In a food processor, add the garlic, ricotta, lemon zest and black pepper and pulse until smooth.
2. Spread ricotta mixture over each bread slices evenly.
3. Press "Power Button" of Ninja Foodi Digital Air Fry Oven and turn the dial to select the "Air Fry" mode.
4. Press the Time button and again turn the dial to set the cooking time to 4 minutes.
5. Now push the Temp button and rotate the dial to set the temperature at 355 degrees F.
6. Press "Start/Pause" button to start.
7. When the unit beeps to show that it is preheated, open the lid and lightly, grease the sheet pan.
8. Arrange the bread slices into "Air Fry Basket" and insert in the oven.
9. Top with egg and bacon pieces and serve.

Nutrition Info: Calories 416 Total Fat 29.2 g Saturated Fat 16.9 g Cholesterol 232 mg Sodium 531 mg Total Carbs 11.2 g Fiber 0.5 g Sugar 2.4 g Protein 27.2 g

Sausage Patties

Servings: 4
Cooking Time: 10 Minutes
Ingredients:

- 1 pack sausage patties
- 1 serving cooking spray

Directions:

1. Preheat your air fryer to 200 degrees C or 400 degrees F.
2. Keep the sausage patties in a basket. Work in batches if needed.
3. Cook for 3 minutes.
4. Turn the sausage over and cook for another 2 minutes.

Nutrition Info: Calories 168, Carbohydrates 1g, Cholesterol 46mg, Total Fat 12g, Protein 14g, Fiber 0g, Sodium 393mg, Sugars 1g

Sausage With Eggs & Avocado

Servings: 2
Cooking Time: 10 Minutes

Ingredients:

- 1 tablespoon maple syrup
- 1 tablespoon balsamic vinegar
- 4 cooked chicken sausages
- 2 hard-boiled eggs, peeled
- 1 small avocado, peeled, pitted and sliced

Directions:

1. In a bowl, mix together the maple syrup and vinegar.
2. Coat the sausages with vinegar mixture.
3. Line the "Sheet Pan" with a lightly, grease piece of foil.
4. Arrange the sausages into the prepared "Sheet Pan".
5. Press "Power Button" of Ninja Foodi Digital Air Fry Oven and turn the dial to select the "Air Roast" mode.
6. Press the Time button and again turn the dial to set the cooking time to 10 minutes.
7. Now push the Temp button and rotate the dial to set the temperature at 450 degrees F.
8. Press "Start/Pause" button to start.
9. When the unit beeps to show that it is preheated, open the lid and insert "Sheet Pan" in the oven.
10. Flip the sausages and coat with the remaining syrup mixture once halfway through.
11. Divide the sausages, eggs and avocado slices onto serving plates and serve.

Nutrition Info: Calories 490 Total Fat 32 g Saturated Fat 8.9 g Cholesterol 164mg Sodium 666 mg Total Carbs 22.1 g Fiber 4.7 g Sugar 7.2 g Protein 26.1 g

Bell Pepper Omelet

Servings: 2
Cooking Time: 10 Minutes

Ingredients:

- 1 teaspoon butter
- 1 small onion, sliced
- ½ of green bell pepper, seeded and chopped
- 4 eggs
- ¼ teaspoon milk
- Salt and ground black pepper, as required
- ¼ cup Cheddar cheese, grated

Directions:

1. In a skillet, melt the butter over medium heat and cook the onion and bell pepper for about 4-5 minutes.
2. Remove the skillet from heat and set aside to cool slightly.
3. Meanwhile, in a bowl, add the eggs, milk, salt and black pepper and beat well.
4. Add the cooked onion mixture and gently, stir to combine.
5. Place the zucchini mixture into a small baking pan.
6. Press "Power Button" of Ninja Foodi Digital Air Fry Oven and turn the dial to select the "Air Fry" mode.
7. Press the Time button and again turn the dial to set the cooking time to 5 minutes.
8. Now push the Temp button and rotate the dial to set the temperature at 355 degrees F.
9. Press "Start/Pause" button to start.
10. When the unit beeps to show that it is preheated, open the lid.
11. Arrange pan over the "Wire Rack" and insert in the oven.
12. Cut the omelet into 2 portions and serve hot.

Nutrition Info: Calories 223 Total Fat 15.5 g Saturated Fat 6.9 g Cholesterol 347 mg Sodium 304 mg Total Carbs 6.4 g Fiber 1.2 g Sugar 3.8 g Protein 15.3 g

Cinnamon And Sugar Doughnuts

Servings: 9
Cooking Time: 16 Minutes

Ingredients:

- 1 teaspoon cinnamon
- 1/3 cup of white sugar
- 2 large egg yolks
- 2-1/2 tablespoons of butter, room temperature
- 1-1/2 teaspoons baking powder
- 2-1/4 cups of all-purpose flour

Directions:

1. Take a bowl and press your butter and white sugar together in it.
2. Add the egg yolks. Stir till it combines well.
3. Now sift the baking powder, flour, and salt in another bowl.
4. Keep one-third of the flour mix and half of the sour cream into your egg-sugar mixture. Stir till it combines well.
5. Now mix the remaining sour cream and flour. Refrigerate till you can use it.
6. Bring together the cinnamon and one-third sugar in your bowl.
7. Roll half-inch-thick dough.
8. Cut large slices (9) in this dough. Create a small circle in the center. This will make doughnut shapes.
9. Preheat your fryer to 175 degrees C or 350 degrees F.
10. Brush melted butter on both sides of your doughnut.
11. Keep half of the doughnuts in the air fryer's basket.
12. Apply the remaining butter on the cooked doughnuts.
13. Dip into the sugar-cinnamon mix immediately.

Nutrition Info: Calories 336, Carbohydrates 44g, Cholesterol 66mg, Total Fat 16g, Protein 4g, Fiber 1g, Sodium 390mg, Sugars 19g

FISH & SEAFOOD RECIPES
Seasoned Catfish

Servings: 4
Cooking Time: 23 Minutes
Ingredients:
- 4 (4-ounce) catfish fillets
- 2 tablespoons Italian seasoning
- Salt and freshly ground black pepper, to taste
- 1 tablespoon olive oil
- 1 tablespoon fresh parsley, chopped

Directions:
1. Rub the fish fillets with seasoning, salt and black pepper generously and then coat with oil.
2. Press "Power Button" of Ninja Foodi Digital Air Fry Oven and turn the dial to select "Air Fry" mode.
3. Press "Time Button" and again turn the dial to set the cooking time to 20 minutes.
4. Now push "Temp Button" and rotate the dial to set the temperature at 400 degrees F.
5. Press "Start/Pause" button to start.
6. When the unit beeps to show that it is preheated, open the lid and grease the air fry basket.
7. Arrange the fish fillets into the prepared air fry basket and insert in the oven.
8. Flip the fish fillets once halfway through.
9. When cooking time is complete, open the lid and transfer the fillets onto serving plates.
10. Serve hot with the garnishing of parsley.
11. Serving Suggestions: Quinoa salad will be a great choice for serving.
12. Variation Tip: Season the fish according to your choice.

Nutrition Info: Calories: 205 Fat: 14.2g Sat Fat: 2.4g Carbohydrates: 0.8g Fiber: 0g Sugar: 0.6g Protein: 17.7g

Tartar Sauce Fish Sticks

Servings: 4
Cooking Time: 15 Minutes
Ingredients:
- 1 oz. fillets of cod, cut into small sticks
- ¾ cup mayonnaise
- 1-1/2 cups bread crumbs
- 2 tablespoons of dill pickle relish
- 1 teaspoon seafood seasoning

Directions:
1. Combine the relish, seafood seasoning, and the mayonnaise in a bowl.
2. Include the fish. Stir gently to coat.
3. Preheat your air fryer to 200 degrees C or 400 degrees F.
4. Keep the bread crumbs on your plate.
5. Coat the sticks of fish in the crumbs one at a time.
6. Transfer the fish sticks to your air fryer basket. Place in one single layer. They shouldn't be touching each other.
7. Cook for 10 minutes.
8. Take out from the basket. Set aside for a minute.
9. Keep in a plate lined with a paper towel before serving.

Nutrition Info: Calories 491, Carbohydrates 30g, Cholesterol 16mg, Total Fat 39g, Protein 5g, Sugar 1g, Fiber 0.2g, Sodium 634mg

Air Fryer Salmon

Servings: 2
Cooking Time: 6 Minutes
Ingredients:
- 5 oz. filets of salmon
- ¼ cup mayonnaise
- ¼ cup of pistachios, chopped finely
- 1-1/2 tablespoons of minced dill
- 2 tablespoons of lemon juice

Directions:
1. Preheat your air fryer to 400 degrees F.
2. Spray olive oil on the basket.
3. Season your salmon with pepper to taste. You can also apply the all-purpose seasoning.
4. Combine the mayonnaise, lemon juice, and dill in a bowl.
5. Pour a spoonful on the fillets.
6. Top the fillets with chopped pistachios. Be generous.
7. Spray olive oil on the salmon lightly.
8. Air fry your fillets now for 5 minutes.
9. Take out the salmon carefully with a spatula from your air fryer.
10. Keep on a plate. Garnish with dill.

Nutrition Info: Calories 305, Carbohydrates 1g, Cholesterol 43mg, Total Fat 21g, Protein 28g, Fiber 2g, Sugar 3g, Sodium 92mg

Lemon Dill Mahi Mahi

Servings: 2
Cooking Time: 15 Minutes
Ingredients:
- 2 fillets of Mahi Mahi, thawed
- 2 lemon slices
- 1 tablespoon olive oil
- 1 tablespoon lemon juice
- 1 tablespoon dill, chopped

Directions:
1. Combine the olive oil and lemon juice in a bowl. Stir.
2. Keep the fish fillets on a parchment paper sheet.
3. Brush the lemon juice mix on each side. Coat heavily.
4. Season with pepper and salt.
5. Add the chopped dill on top.
6. Keep the fillets of Mahi Mahi in your air fryer basket.
7. Cook at 400° F for 12 minutes.
8. Take out. Serve immediately.

Nutrition Info: Calories 95, Carbohydrates 2g, Cholesterol 21mg, Total Fat 7g, Protein 6g, Sugar 0.2g, Sodium 319mg

Herbed Salmon

Servings: 2
Cooking Time: 10 Minutes
Ingredients:
- 1 tablespoon fresh lime juice
- ½ tablespoons olive oil
- Salt and freshly ground black pepper, to taste
- 1 garlic clove, minced
- ½ teaspoon fresh thyme leaves, chopped
- ½ teaspoon fresh rosemary, chopped
- 2 (7-ounce) salmon fillets

Directions:
1. In a bowl, add all the ingredients except the salmon and mix well.
2. Add the salmon fillets and coat with the mixture generously.
3. Press "Power Button" of Ninja Foodi Digital Air Fry Oven and turn the dial to select "Air Bake" mode.
4. Press "Time Button" and again turn the dial to set the cooking time to 10 minutes.
5. Now push "Temp Button" and rotate the dial to set the temperature at 400 degrees F.
6. Press "Start/Pause" button to start.
7. When the unit beeps to show that it is preheated, open the lid.
8. Arrange the salmon fillets over the greased wire rack and insert in the oven.
9. Flip the fillets once halfway through.
10. When cooking time is complete, open the lid and transfer the salmon fillets onto serving plates.
11. Serve hot.
12. Serving Suggestions: Serve with steamed asparagus.
13. Variation Tip: For best result, use freshly squeezed lime juice.

Nutrition Info: Calories: 297 Fat: 15.8g Sat Fat: 2.3g Carbohydrates: 0.9g Fiber: 0.3g Sugar: 0g Protein: 38.6g

Crumbed Fish

Servings: 4
Cooking Time: 12 Minutes
Ingredients:
- 4 flounder fillets
- 1 cup bread crumbs
- 1 egg, beaten
- ¼ cup of vegetable oil
- 1 lemon, sliced

Directions:
1. Preheat your air fryer to 180 degrees C or 350 degrees F.
2. Mix the oil and bread crumbs in a bowl. Keep stirring until you see this mixture becoming crumbly and loose.
3. Now dip your fish fillets into the egg. Remove any excess.
4. Dip your fillets into the bread crumb mix. Make sure to coat evenly.
5. Keep the coated fillets in your preheated fryer gently.
6. Cook until you see the fish flaking easily with a fork.
7. Add lemon slices for garnishing.

Nutrition Info: Calories 389, Carbohydrates 23g, Cholesterol 107mg, Total Fat 21g, Protein 27g, Fiber 3g, Sodium 309mg, Sugars 2g

Pesto Salmon

Servings: 4
Cooking Time: 15 Minutes
Ingredients:
- 1¼ pound salmon fillet, cut into 4 fillets
- 2 tablespoons white wine
- 1 tablespoon fresh lemon juice
- 2 tablespoons pesto, thawed
- 2 tablespoons pine nuts, toasted

Directions:
1. Arrange the salmon fillets onto q foil-lined baking pan, skin-side down.
2. Drizzle the salmon fillets with wine and lemon juice.
3. Set aside for about 15 minutes.
4. Spread pesto over each salmon fillet evenly.
5. Press "Power Button" of Ninja Foodi Digital Air Fry Oven and turn the dial to select the "Air Broil" mode.
6. Press the Time button and again turn the dial to set the cooking time to 15 minutes.
7. Press "Start/Pause" button to start.
8. When the unit beeps to show that it is preheated, open the lid.
9. Insert the baking pan in oven.
10. Garnish with toasted pine nuts and serve.

Nutrition Info: Calories 257 Total Fat 15 g Saturated Fat 2.1 g Cholesterol 64 mg Sodium 111 mg Total Carbs 1.3 g Fiber 0.3 g Sugar 0.8 g Protein 28.9 g

Buttered Salmon

Servings: 2
Cooking Time: 10 Minutes
Ingredients:
- 2 (6-ounce) salmon fillets
- Salt and freshly ground black pepper, to taste
- 1 tablespoon butter, melted

Directions:
1. Season each salmon fillet with salt and black pepper and then, coat with the butter.
2. Press "Power Button" of Ninja Foodi Digital Air Fry Oven and turn the dial to select "Air Fry" mode.
3. Press "Time Button" and again turn the dial to set the cooking time to 10 minutes.
4. Now push "Temp Button" and rotate the dial to set the temperature at 360 degrees F.
5. Press "Start/Pause" button to start.
6. When the unit beeps to show that it is preheated, open the lid and grease the air fry basket.
7. Arrange the salmon fillets into the prepared air fry basket and insert in the oven.
8. When cooking time is complete, open the lid and transfer the salmon fillets onto serving plates.
9. Serve hot.
10. Serving Suggestions: Enjoy with roasted parsnip puree.
11. Variation Tip: Salmon should look bright and shiny.

Nutrition Info: Calories: 276 Fat: 16.3g Sat Fat: 5.2g Carbohydrates: 0g Fiber: 0g Sugar: 0g Protein: 33.1g

Herbed Scallops

Servings: 2
Cooking Time: 14 Minutes

Ingredients:

- ¾ pound sea scallops, cleaned and pat dry
- 1 tablespoon butter, melted
- ¼ tablespoon fresh thyme, minced
- ¼ tablespoon fresh rosemary, minced
- Salt and freshly ground black pepper, to taste

Directions:

1. In a large bowl, place the scallops, butter, herbs, salt, and black pepper and toss to coat well.
2. Press "Power Button" of Ninja Foodi Digital Air Fry Oven and turn the dial to select "Air Fry" mode.
3. Press "Time Button" and again turn the dial to set the cooking time to 4 minutes.
4. Now push "Temp Button" and rotate the dial to set the temperature at 390 degrees F.
5. Press "Start/Pause" button to start.
6. When the unit beeps to show that it is preheated, open the lid and grease the air fry basket.
7. Arrange the scallops into the air fry basket and insert in the oven.
8. When cooking time is complete, open the lid and transfer the scallops onto serving plates.
9. Serve hot.
10. Serving Suggestions: Potato fries will be great with these scallops.
11. Variation Tip: Remove the side muscles from the scallops.

Nutrition Info: Calories: 203 Fat: 7.1g Sat Fat: 3.8g Carbohydrates: 4.5g Fiber: 0.3g Sugar: 0g Protein: 28.7g

Spiced Tilapia

Servings: 2
Cooking Time: 12 Minutes
Ingredients:
- ¼ teaspoon garlic powder
- ¼ teaspoon onion powder
- ¼ teaspoon ground cumin
- Salt and ground black pepper, as required
- 2 (6-ounce) tilapia fillets
- 1 tablespoon butter, melted

Directions:
1. In a small bowl, mix together the spices, salt and black pepper.
2. Coat the tilapia fillets with oil and then rub with spice mixture.
3. Press "Power Button" of Ninja Foodi Digital Air Fry Oven and turn the dial to select the "Air Fry" mode.
4. Press the Time button and again turn the dial to set the cooking time to 12 minutes.
5. Now push the Temp button and rotate the dial to set the temperature at 360 degrees F.
6. Press "Start/Pause" button to start.
7. When the unit beeps to show that it is preheated, open the lid.
8. Arrange the tilapia fillets over the greased "Wire Rack" and insert in the oven.
9. Flip the tilapia fillets once halfway through.
10. Serve hot.

Nutrition Info: Calories 194 Total Fat 7.4 g Saturated Fat 4.3 g Cholesterol 98 mg Sodium 179 mg Total Carbs 0.6 g Fiber 0.1 g Sugar 0.2 g Protein 31.8 g

Crusted Sole

Servings: 2
Cooking Time: 15 Minutes

Ingredients:

- 2 teaspoons mayonnaise
- 1 teaspoon fresh chives, minced
- 3 tablespoons Parmesan cheese, shredded
- 2 tablespoons panko breadcrumbs
- Salt and freshly ground black pepper, to taste
- 2 (4-ounce) sole fillets

Directions:

1. In a shallow dish, mix together the mayonnaise and chives.
2. In another shallow dish, mix together the cheese, breadcrumbs, salt and black pepper.
3. Coat the fish fillets with mayonnaise mixture and then roll in cheese mixture.
4. Arrange the sole fillets onto the greased sheet pan in a single layer.
5. Press "Power Button" of Ninja Foodi Digital Air Fry Oven and turn the dial to select "Air Bake" mode.
6. Press "Time Button" and again turn the dial to set the cooking time to 15 minutes.
7. Now push "Temp Button" and rotate the dial to set the temperature at 450 degrees F.
8. Press "Start/Pause" button to start.
9. When the unit beeps to show that it is preheated, open the lid and insert the sheet pan in the oven.
10. When cooking time is complete, open the lid and transfer the fish fillets onto serving plates.
11. Serve hot.
12. Serving Suggestions: Roasted potatoes make a great side for fish.
13. Variation Tip: If you want a gluten-free option then use pork rinds instead of breadcrumbs.

Nutrition Info: Calories: 584 Fat: 14.6g Sat Fat: 5.2g Carbohydrates: 16.7g Fiber: 0.4g Sugar: 0.2g Protein: 33.2g

Buttered Trout

Servings: 2

Cooking Time: 10 Minutes

Ingredients:

- 2 (6-ounces) trout fillets
- Salt and ground black pepper, as required
- 1 tablespoon butter, melted

Directions:

1. Season each trout fillet with salt and black pepper and then, coat with the butter.
2. Arrange the trout fillets onto the greased "Sheet Pan" in a single layer.
3. Press "Power Button" of Ninja Foodi Digital Air Fry Oven and turn the dial to select the "Air Fry" mode.
4. Press the Time button and again turn the dial to set the cooking time to 10 minutes.
5. Now push the Temp button and rotate the dial to set the temperature at 360 degrees F.
6. Press "Start/Pause" button to start.
7. When the unit beeps to show that it is preheated, open the lid.
8. Insert the "Sheet Pan" in oven.
9. Flip the fillets once halfway through.
10. Serve hot.

Nutrition Info: Calories 374 Total Fat 20.2 g Saturated Fat 6.2 g Cholesterol 141 mg Sodium 232 mg Total Carbs 0 g Fiber 0 g Sugar 0 g Protein 45.4 g

Zesty Fish Fillets

Servings: 4

Cooking Time: 12 Minutes

Ingredients:

- 4 fillets of salmon or tilapia
- 2-1/2 teaspoons vegetable oil
- ¾ cups crushed cornflakes or bread crumbs
- 2 eggs, beaten
- 1 packet dry dressing mix

Directions:

1. Preheat the air fryer to 180° C.
2. Mix the dressing mix and the breadcrumbs together.
3. Pour the oil. Stir until you see the mix getting crumbly and loose.
4. Now dip your fish fillets into the egg. Remove the excess.
5. Dip your fillets into the crumb mix. Coat evenly.
6. Transfer to the fryer carefully.
7. Cook for 10 minutes. Take out and serve.
8. You can also add some lemon wedges on your fish.

Nutrition Info: Calories 382, Carbohydrates 8g, Cholesterol 166mg, Total Fat 22g, Protein 38g, Sodium 220mg, Calcium 50mg

Sweet & Tangy Herring

Servings: 2
Cooking Time: 12 Minutes
Ingredients:
- 2 (5-ounce) herring fillets
- 1 garlic clove, minced
- 1 teaspoon fresh rosemary, minced
- 1 tablespoon butter, melted
- 1 tablespoon balsamic vinegar
- ¼ teaspoon maple syrup
- 1/8 teaspoon Sriracha

Directions:
1. In a large resealable bag, place all the ingredients and seal the bag.
2. Shake the bag well to mix.
3. Place the bag in the refrigerator to marinate for at least 30 minutes.
4. Remove the fish fillets from bag and shake off the excess marinade.
5. Arrange the fish fillets onto the greased sheet pan in a single layer.
6. Press "Power Button" of Ninja Foodi Digital Air Fry Oven and turn the dial to select "Air Bake" mode.
7. Press "Time Button" and again turn the dial to set the cooking time to 12 minutes.
8. Now push "Temp Button" and rotate the dial to set the temperature at 450 degrees F.
9. Press "Start/Pause" button to start.
10. When the unit beeps to show that it is preheated, open the lid and insert the sheet pan in the oven.
11. Flip the fillets once halfway through.
12. When cooking time is complete, open the lid and transfer the fillets onto serving plates.
13. Serve hot.
14. Serving Suggestions: Enjoy with grilled vegetables.
15. Variation Tip: Use unsalted butter.

Nutrition Info: Calories: 347 Fat: 22.3g Sat Fat: 7.4g Carbohydrates: 1.6g Fiber: 0.3g Sugar: 0.5g Protein: 32.8g

Crusted Salmon

Servings: 2

Cooking Time: 15 Minutes

Ingredients:

- 2 (6-ounce) skinless salmon fillets
- Salt and ground black pepper, as required
- 3 tablespoons walnuts, chopped finely
- 3 tablespoons quick-cooking oats, crushed
- 2 tablespoons olive oil

Directions:

1. Rub the salmon fillets with salt and black pepper evenly.
2. In a bowl, mix together the walnuts, oats and oil.
3. Arrange the salmon fillets onto the greased "Sheet Pan" in a single layer.
4. Place the oat mixture over salmon fillets and gently, press down.
5. Press "Power Button" of Ninja Foodi Digital Air Fry Oven and turn the dial to select the "Air Bake" mode.
6. Press the Time button and again turn the dial to set the cooking time to 15 minutes.
7. Now push the Temp button and rotate the dial to set the temperature at 400 degrees F.
8. Press "Start/Pause" button to start.
9. When the unit beeps to show that it is preheated, open the lid.
10. Insert the "Sheet Pan" in oven.
11. Serve hot.

Nutrition Info: Calories 446 Total Fat 31.9 g Saturated Fat 4 g Cholesterol 75 mg Sodium 153 mg Total Carbs 6.4 g Fiber 1.6 g Sugar 0.2 g Protein 36.8 g

Green Beans With Southern Catfish

Servings: 2

Cooking Time: 10 Minutes

Ingredients:

- 2 catfish fillets
- ¾ oz. green beans, trimmed
- 1 large egg, beaten lightly
- 2 tablespoons of mayonnaise
- 1 teaspoon light brown sugar
- 1/3 cup breadcrumbs
- ½ teaspoon of apple cider vinegar

Directions:

1. Keep the green beans in a bowl. Apply cooking spray liberally.
2. Sprinkle some brown sugar, a pint of salt, and crushed red pepper (optional).
3. Keep in your air fryer basket. Cook at 400 degrees F until it becomes tender and brown.
4. Transfer to your bowl. Use aluminum foil to cover.
5. Toss the catfish in flour. Shake off the excesses.
6. Dip the pieces into the egg. Coat all sides evenly. Sprinkle breadcrumbs.
7. Keep fish in the fryer basket. Apply cooking spray.
8. Now cook at 400 degrees F until it is cooked thoroughly and brown.
9. Sprinkle pepper and ¼ teaspoon of salt.
10. Whisk together the vinegar, sugar, and mayonnaise in a bowl.
11. Serve the fish with tartar sauce and green beans.

Nutrition Info: Calories 562, Carbohydrates 31g, Total Fat 34g, Protein 33g, Fiber 7g, Sugar 16g, Sodium 677mg

Fish Sticks

Servings: 4
Cooking Time: 10 Minutes

Ingredients:

- 16 oz. fillets of tilapia or cod
- 1 egg
- ¼ cup all-purpose flour
- ¼ cup Parmesan cheese, grated
- 1 teaspoon of paprika
- ½ cup bread crumbs

Directions:

1. Preheat your air fryer to 200 degrees C or 400 degrees F.
2. Use paper towels to pat dry your fish.
3. Cut into 1 x 3-inch sticks.
4. Keep flour in a dish. Beat the egg in another dish.
5. Bring together the paprika, cheese, bread crumbs and some pepper in another shallow dish.
6. Coat the sticks of fish in flour.
7. Now dip them in the egg and coat the bread crumbs mix.
8. Apply cooking spray on the air fryer basket.
9. Keep the sticks in your basket. They shouldn't touch.
10. Apply cooking spray on each fish stick.
11. Cook in the air fryer for 3 minutes. Flip over and cook for another 2 minutes.

Nutrition Info: Calories 217, Carbohydrates 17g, Cholesterol 92mg, Total Fat 5g, Protein 26g, Fiber 0.7g, Sugar 0g, Sodium 245mg

Ranch Tilapia

Servings: 4
Cooking Time: 13 Minutes
Ingredients:
- ¾ cup cornflakes, crushed
- 1 (1-ounce) packet dry ranch-style dressing mix
- 2½ tablespoons vegetable oil
- 2 eggs
- 4 (6-ounce) tilapia fillets

Directions:
1. In a shallow bowl, crack the eggs and beat slightly.
2. In another bowl, add the cornflakes, ranch dressing, and oil and mix until a crumbly mixture forms.
3. Dip the fish fillets into egg and then, coat with the breadcrumbs mixture.
4. Press "Power Button" of Ninja Foodi Digital Air Fry Oven and turn the dial to select "Air Fry" mode.
5. Press "Time Button" and again turn the dial to set the cooking time to 13 minutes.
6. Now push "Temp Button" and rotate the dial to set the temperature at 356 degrees F.
7. Press "Start/Pause" button to start.
8. When the unit beeps to show that it is preheated, open the lid and grease the air fry basket.
9. Arrange the tilapia fillets into the prepared air fry basket and insert in the oven. When cooking time is complete, open the lid and transfer the fillets onto serving plates.
10. Serve hot.
11. Serving Suggestions: Serve tilapia with lemon butter.
12. Variation Tip: The skin should be removed, either before cooking or before serving.

Nutrition Info: Calories: 267 Fat: 12.2g Sat Fat: 3g Carbohydrates: 5.1g Fiber: 0.2g Sugar: 0.9g Protein: 34.9g

Glazed Salmon

Servings: 2

Cooking Time: 8 Minutes

Ingredients:

- 2 (6-ounce) salmon fillets
- Salt, to taste
- 2 tablespoons honey

Directions:

1. Sprinkle the salmon fillets with salt and then coat with honey.
2. Press "Power Button" of Ninja Foodi Digital Air Fry Oven and turn the dial to select "Air Fry" mode.
3. Press "Time Button" and again turn the dial to set the cooking time to 8 minutes.
4. Now push "Temp Button" and rotate the dial to set the temperature at 355 degrees F.
5. Press "Start/Pause" button to start.
6. When the unit beeps to show that it is preheated, open the lid and grease the air fry basket.
7. Arrange the salmon fillets into the prepared air fry basket and insert in the oven.
8. When cooking time is complete, open the lid and transfer the salmon fillets onto serving plates.
9. Serve hot.
10. Serving Suggestions: Fresh baby greens will be great if served with glazed salmon.
11. Variation Tip: honey can be replaced with maple syrup too.

Nutrition Info: Calories: 289 Fat: 10.5g Sat Fat: 1.5g Carbohydrates: 17.3g Fiber: 0g Sugar: 17.3g Protein: 33.1g

Lemony Shrimp

Servings: 3
Cooking Time: 8 Minutes
Ingredients:
- 2 tablespoons fresh lemon juice
- 1 tablespoon olive oil
- 1 teaspoon lemon pepper
- ¼ teaspoon paprika
- ¼ teaspoon garlic powder
- 12 ounces medium shrimp, peeled and deveined

Directions:
1. In a large bowl, add all the ingredients except the shrimp and mix until well combined.
2. Add the shrimp and toss to coat well.
3. Arrange the shrimps onto a sheet pan.
4. Press "Power Button" of Ninja Foodi Digital Air Fry Oven and turn the dial to select "Air Fry" mode.
5. Press "Time Button" and again turn the dial to set the cooking time to 8 minutes.
6. Now push "Temp Button" and rotate the dial to set the temperature at 400 degrees F.
7. Press "Start/Pause" button to start.
8. When the unit beeps to show that it is preheated, open the lid and insert the sheet pan in the oven.
9. When cooking time is complete, open the lid and transfer the shrimp onto serving plates.
10. Serve hot.
11. Serving Suggestions: Serve with scalloped potatoes.
12. Variation Tip: Avoid shrimp that smell like ammonia.

Nutrition Info: Calories: 164 Fat: 6.1g Sat Fat: 0.8g Carbohydrates: 0.9g Fiber: 0.3g Sugar: 0.3g Protein: 24.5g

Grilled Fish Fillet In Pesto Sauce

Servings: 2
Cooking Time: 8 Minutes
Ingredients:
- 2 fish fillets, white fish
- 1 tablespoon of olive oil
- 2 cloves of garlic
- 1 bunch basil
- 1 tablespoon Parmesan cheese, grated

Directions:
1. Heat your air fryer to 180 degrees C.
2. Brush oil on your fish fillets. Season with salt and pepper.
3. Keep in your basket and into the fryer.
4. Cook for 6 minutes.
5. Keep the basil leaves with the cheese, olive oil, and garlic in your food processor.
6. Pulse until it becomes a sauce. Include salt to taste.
7. Keep fillets on your serving plate. Serve with pesto sauce.

Nutrition Info: Calories 1453, Carbohydrates 3g, Cholesterol 58mg, Total Fat 141g, Protein 43g, Fiber 1g, Sugar 0g, Sodium 1773mg

POULTRY RECIPES

Egg Frittata

Servings: 2
Cooking Time: 15 Minutes

Ingredients:

- 4 eggs
- ¼ cup baby mushrooms, chopped
- ½ cup of milk
- 2 onions, chopped
- ¼ cup cheddar cheese

Directions:

1. Grease your pan with butter and keep it aside.
2. Whisk together the milk and eggs in a bowl. Blend well.
3. Stir in the mushrooms, onion, cheddar cheese, salt, and pepper. You can also include some hot sauce.
4. Now pour in the egg mix into your pan.
5. Transfer to your air fryer. Cook for 12 minutes at 360 degrees F.

Nutrition Info: Calories 281, Carbohydrates 6g, Cholesterol 348mg, Total Fat 21g, Protein 17g, Sugar 4g, Calcium 229mg, Sodium 826mg

Glazed Chicken Drumsticks

Servings: 4
Cooking Time: 20 Minutes

Ingredients:

- ¼ cup Dijon mustard
- 1 tablespoon maple syrup
- 2 tablespoons olive oil
- 1 tablespoon fresh rosemary, minced
- Salt and freshly ground black pepper, to taste
- 4 (6-ounce) chicken drumsticks

Directions:

1. In a bowl, add all ingredients except the drumsticks and mix until well combined.
2. Add the drumsticks and coat with the mixture generously.
3. Cover the bowl and refrigerate to marinate overnight.
4. Place the chicken drumsticks into the greased baking pan.
5. Press "Power Button" of Ninja Foodi Digital Air Fry Oven and turn the dial to select "Air Fry" mode.
6. Press "Time Button" and again turn the dial to set the cooking time to 12 minutes.
7. Now push "Temp Button" and rotate the dial to set the temperature at 320 degrees F.
8. Press "Start/Pause" button to start.
9. When the unit beeps to show that it is preheated, open the lid and insert baking pan in the oven.
10. After 12 minutes, flip the drumsticks and set the temperature to 390 degrees F for 8 minutes.
11. When cooking time is complete, open the lid and transfer the chicken drumsticks onto serving plates.
12. Serve hot.
13. Serving Suggestions:
14. Variation Tip: You can increase the quantity of maple syrup according to your taste.

Nutrition Info: Calories: 374 Fat: 17.5g Sat Fat: 3.7g Carbohydrates: 4.7g Fiber: 0.9g Sugar: 3.1g Protein: 47.5g

Blackened Chicken Breast

Servings: 2
Cooking Time: 20 Minutes

Ingredients:

- 2 chicken breast halves, skinless and boneless
- 1 teaspoon thyme, ground
- 2 teaspoons of paprika
- 2 teaspoons vegetable oil
- ½ teaspoon onion powder

Directions:

1. Combine the thyme, paprika, onion powder, and salt together in your bowl.
2. Transfer the spice mix to a flat plate.
3. Rub vegetable oil on the chicken breast. Coat fully.
4. Roll the chicken pieces in the spice mixture. Press down, ensuring that all sides have the spice mix.
5. Keep aside for 5 minutes.
6. In the meantime, preheat your air fryer to 175 degrees C or 360 degrees F.
7. Keep the chicken in the air fryer basket. Cook for 8 minutes.
8. Flip once and cook for another 7 minutes.
9. Transfer the breasts to a serving plate. Serve after 5 minutes.

Nutrition Info: Calories 427, Carbohydrates 3g, Cholesterol 198mg, Total Fat 11g, Protein 79g, Sugar 1g, Fiber 2g, Sodium 516mg

Garlicky Duck Legs

Servings: 2
Cooking Time: 30 Minutes

Ingredients:

- 2 garlic cloves, minced
- 1 tablespoon fresh parsley, chopped
- 1 teaspoon five-spice powder
- Salt and freshly ground black pepper, to taste
- 2 duck legs

Directions:

1. In a bowl, mix together the garlic, parsley, five-spice powder, salt and black pepper.
2. Rub the duck legs with garlic mixture generously.
3. Arrange the duck legs onto the greased sheet pan.
4. Press "Power Button" of Ninja Foodi Digital Air Fry Oven and turn the dial to select "Air Fry" mode.
5. Press "Time Button" and again turn the dial to set the cooking time to 30 minutes.
6. Now push "Temp Button" and rotate the dial to set the temperature at 340 degrees F.
7. Press "Start/Pause" button to start.
8. When the unit beeps to show that it is preheated, open the lid and insert the sheet pan in the oven.
9. Flip the duck legs once halfway through.
10. When cooking time is complete, open the lid and transfer the duck legs onto serving plates.
11. Serve hot.
12. Serving Suggestions: Serve these duck legs with cucmber salad.
13. Variation Tip: Never defrost the duck meat on the counter.

Nutrition Info: Calories: 434 Fat: 14.4g Sat Fat: 3.2g Carbohydrates: 1.1g Fiber: 0.1g Sugar: 0.1g Protein: 70.4g

Nashville Chicken

Servings: 8

Cooking Time: 20 Minutes

Ingredients:

- 2 oz. chicken breast, boneless
- 2 tablespoons hot sauce
- ½ cup of olive oil
- 3 large eggs
- 3 cups all-purpose flour
- 1 teaspoon of chili powder
- 1-1/2 cups buttermilk

Directions:

1. Toss together the chicken, hot sauce, salt, and pepper in a bowl. Combine well.
2. Cover and refrigerate for three hours.
3. Pour flour into your bowl.
4. Now whisk the buttermilk and eggs together. Add 1 tablespoon of hot sauce.
5. For dredging your chicken, keep it in the flour first. Toss evenly for coating.
6. Keep it in your buttermilk mix. Then into the flour.
7. Keep them on your baking sheet.
8. Set the air fryer at 380 degrees. Place the tenders in your fryer.
9. Cook for 10 minutes.
10. For the sauce, whisk the spices and olive oil. Combine well.
11. Pour over the fried chicken immediately.

Nutrition Info: Calories 668, Carbohydrates 44g, Cholesterol 156mg, Total Fat 40g, Protein 33g, Sugar 5g, Fiber 2g, Sodium 847mg

Peruvian Chicken Drumsticks & Green Crema

Servings: 6
Cooking Time: 15 Minutes
Ingredients:
- 6 chicken drumsticks
- 2 garlic cloves, grated
- 1 tablespoon of olive oil
- 1 tablespoon honey
- 1 cup of baby spinach leaves, with stems removed
- ¼ cup cilantro leaves
- ¾ cup of sour cream

Directions:
1. Bring together the honey, garlic, pepper, and salt in a bowl.
2. Add the drumsticks. Coat well by tossing.
3. Keep the drumsticks in a vertical position in the basket. Keep them leaning against the wall of the basket.
4. Cook in your air fryer at 200 degrees C or 400 degrees F for 15 minutes.
5. In the meantime, combine the sour cream, cilantro leaves, pepper and salt in a food processor bowl.
6. Process until the crema has become smooth.
7. Drizzle the crema sauce over your drumsticks.

Nutrition Info: Calories 337, Carbohydrates 6g, Cholesterol 82mg, Total Fat 25g, Protein 22g, Sugar 3g, Fiber 0.5g, Sodium 574mg

Crispy Roasted Chicken

Servings: 7
Cooking Time: 40 Minutes

Ingredients:

- 1 (3½-pound) whole chicken, cut into 8 pieces
- Salt and ground black pepper, as required
- 2 cups buttermilk
- 2 cups all-purpose flour
- 1 tablespoon ground mustard
- 1 tablespoon garlic powder
- 1 tablespoon onion powder
- 1 tablespoon paprika

Directions:

1. Rub the chicken pieces with salt and black pepper.
2. In a large bowl, add the chicken pieces and buttermilk and refrigerate to marinate for at least 1 hour.
3. Meanwhile, in a large bowl, place the flour, mustard, spices, salt and black pepper and mix well.
4. Grease the cooking racks generously.
5. Remove the chicken pieces from bowl and drip off the excess buttermilk.
6. Coat the chicken pieces with the flour mixture, shaking any excess off.
7. Press "Power Button" of Ninja Foodi Digital Air Fry Oven and turn the dial to select the "Air Fry" mode.
8. Press the Time button and again turn the dial to set the cooking time to 20 minutes.
9. Now push the Temp button and rotate the dial to set the temperature at 390 degrees F.
10. Press "Start/Pause" button to start.
11. When the unit beeps to show that it is preheated, open the lid and grease "Air Fry Basket".
12. Arrange half of the chicken pieces into "Air Fry Basket" and insert in the oven.
13. Repeat with the remaining chicken pieces.
14. Serve immediately.

Nutrition Info: Calories 518 Total Fat 8.5 g Saturated Fat 2.4 g Cholesterol 177 mg Sodium 242 mg Total Carbs 33.4 g Fiber 1.8 g Sugar 4.3 g Protein 72.6 g

Roasted Cornish Game Hen

Servings: 4
Cooking Time: 16 Minutes

Ingredients:

- ¼ cup olive oil
- 1 teaspoon fresh rosemary, chopped
- 1 teaspoon fresh thyme, chopped
- 1 teaspoon fresh lemon zest, finely grated
- ¼ teaspoon sugar
- ¼ teaspoon red pepper flakes, crushed
- Salt and freshly ground black pepper, to taste
- 2 pounds Cornish game hen, backbone removed and halved

Directions:

1. In a bowl, mix together oil, herbs, lemon zest, sugar, and spices.
2. Add the hen portions and coat with the marinade generously.
3. Cover and refrigerate for about 24 hours.
4. In a strainer, place the hen portions and set aside to drain any liquid.
5. Press "Power Button" of Ninja Foodi Digital Air Fry Oven and turn the dial to select "Air Fry" mode.
6. Press "Time Button" and again turn the dial to set the cooking time to 16 minutes.
7. Now push "Temp Button" and rotate the dial to set the temperature at 390 degrees F.
8. Press "Start/Pause" button to start.
9. When the unit beeps to show that it is preheated, open the lid and grease the air fry basket.
10. Arrange the hen portions into the prepared basket and insert in the oven.
11. When cooking time is complete, open the lid and transfer the hen portions onto a platter.
12. Cut each portion in half and serve.
13. Serving Suggestions: Serve with dinner rolls.
14. Variation Tip: Place the hens in the basket, breast side up.

Nutrition Info: Calories: 557 Fat: 45.1g Sat Fat: 1.8g Carbohydrates: 0.8g Fiber: 0.3g Sugar: 0.3g Protein: 38.5g

Bacon-wrapped Chicken Breasts

Servings: 4
Cooking Time: 23 Minutes

Ingredients:

- 1 tablespoon palm sugar
- 6-7 Fresh basil leaves
- 2 tablespoons fish sauce
- 2 tablespoons water
- 2 (8-ounces) chicken breasts, cut each breast in half horizontally
- Salt and freshly ground black pepper, to taste
- 12 bacon strips
- 1½ teaspoon honey

Directions:

1. In a small heavy-bottomed pan, add palm sugar over medium-low heat and cook for about 2-3 minutes or until caramelized, stirring continuously.
2. Add the basil, fish sauce and water and stir to combine.
3. Remove from heat and transfer the sugar mixture into a large bowl.
4. Sprinkle each chicken breast with salt and black pepper.
5. Add the chicken pieces in the sugar mixture and coat generously.
6. Refrigerate to marinate for about 4-6 hours.
7. Wrap each chicken piece with 3 bacon strips.
8. Coat each piece with honey slightly.
9. Press "Power Button" of Ninja Foodi Digital Air Fry Oven and turn the dial to select "Air Fry" mode.
10. Press "Time Button" and again turn the dial to set the cooking time to 20 minutes.
11. Now push "Temp Button" and rotate the dial to set the temperature at 365 degrees F.
12. Press "Start/Pause" button to start.
13. When the unit beeps to show that it is preheated, open the lid and grease the air fry basket.
14. Arrange the chicken breasts into the prepared basket and insert in the oven.
15. Flip the chicken breasts once halfway through.
16. When cooking time is complete, open the lid and transfer the chicken breasts onto serving plates.
17. Serve hot.
18. Serving Suggestions: Serve with balsamic-glazed green beans.
19. Variation Tip: Use thick-cut bacon strips.

Nutrition Info: Calories: 709, Fat: 44.8g, Sat Fat: 14.3g, Carbohydrates: 6.8g, Fiber: 0g Sugar: 4.7g, Protein: 65.6g

Asian Deviled Eggs

Servings: 12
Cooking Time: 15 Minutes

Ingredients:

- 6 eggs
- 2 tablespoons of mayonnaise
- 1 teaspoon soy sauce, low-sodium
- 1-1/2 teaspoons of sesame oil
- 1 teaspoon Dijon mustard

Directions:

1. Keep the eggs on the air fryer rack. Make sure that there is adequate space between them.
2. Set the temperature to 125 degrees C or 160 degrees F.
3. Air fry for 15 minutes.
4. Take out the eggs from your air fryer. Keep in an ice water bowl for 10 minutes.
5. Take them out of the water. Now peel and cut them in half.
6. Scoop out the yolks carefully. Keep in a food processor.
7. Add the sesame oil, mayonnaise, Dijon mustard, and soy sauce.
8. Process until everything combines well. The mixture should be creamy.
9. Fill up your piping bag with this yolk mixture. Distribute evenly into the egg whites. They should be heaping full.
10. You can garnish with green onions and sesame seeds (optional).

Nutrition Info: Calories 70, Carbohydrates 1g, Cholesterol 94mg, Total Fat 6g, Protein 3g, Sugar 0g, Fiber 0.1g, Sodium 102mg

Herbed Chicken Drumsticks

Servings: 2
Cooking Time: 20 Minutes
Ingredients:
- 1 tablespoon olive oil
- ½ teaspoon dried thyme, crushed
- ½ teaspoon dried rosemary, crushed
- ½ teaspoon oregano, crushed
- Salt and freshly ground black pepper, to taste
- 2 (6-ounce) chicken drumsticks

Directions:
1. In a large bowl, place the oil, herbs, salt and black pepper and mix well.
2. Add the chicken drumsticks and coat with the mixture generously.
3. Place the chicken drumsticks into the greased baking pan.
4. Press "Power Button" of Ninja Foodi Digital Air Fry Oven and turn the dial to select "Air Fry" mode.
5. Press "Time Button" and again turn the dial to set the cooking time to 20 minutes.
6. Now push "Temp Button" and rotate the dial to set the temperature at 375 degrees F.
7. Press "Start/Pause" button to start.
8. When the unit beeps to show that it is preheated, open the lid and insert the baking pan in the oven.
9. When cooking time is complete, open the lid and transfer the chicken drumsticks onto serving plates.
10. Serve hot.
11. Serving Suggestions: Any kind of dipping sauce will be great for these drumsticks.
12. Variation Tip: You can use fresh herbs instead of dried herbs.

Nutrition Info: Calories: 350 Fat: 16.8g Sat Fat: 3.6g Carbohydrates: 0.6g Fiber: 0.4g Sugar: 0g Protein: 46.9g

Herbed Roasted Chicken

Servings: 6
Cooking Time: 1 Hour 10 Minutes

Ingredients:

- ¼ cup butter, softened
- 1 teaspoon dried rosemary, crushed
- 1 teaspoon dried basil, crushed
- 1 teaspoon dried oregano, crushed
- 1 teaspoon dried thyme, crushed
- 1 tablespoon garlic powder
- 1 tablespoon paprika
- 1 tablespoon ground cumin
- Salt and freshly ground black pepper, to taste
- 1 (3-pound) whole chicken, neck and giblets removed

Directions:

1. In a bowl, add the butter, herbs, spices and salt and mix well.
2. Rub the chicken with spice mixture generously.
3. With kitchen twine, tie off wings and legs.
4. Arrange the chicken onto the greased sheet pan.
5. Press "Power Button" of Ninja Foodi Digital Air Fry Oven and turn the dial to select "Air Bake" mode.
6. Press "Time Button" and again turn the dial to set the cooking time to 70 minutes.
7. Now push "Temp Button" and rotate the dial to set the temperature at 380 degrees F.
8. Press "Start/Pause" button to start.
9. When the unit beeps to show that it is preheated, open the lid and insert the sheet pan in oven.
10. When cooking time is complete, open the lid and place the chicken onto a platter for about 10-15 minutes before carving.
11. With a sharp knife, cut the chicken into desired sized pieces and serve.
12. Serving Suggestions: Roasted vegetables will accompany this roasted chicken nicely.
13. Variation Tip: Rub the chicken with your hands for even coating.

Nutrition Info: Calories: 434 Fat: 15g Sat Fat: 6.9g Carbohydrates: 2.5g Fiber: 0.9g Sugar: 0.5g Protein: 66.4g

Herbed & Spiced Turkey Breast

Servings: 6
Cooking Time: 40 Minutes
Ingredients:
- ¼ cup butter, softened
- 2 tablespoons fresh rosemary, chopped
- 2 tablespoon fresh thyme, chopped
- 2 tablespoons fresh sage, chopped
- 2 tablespoons fresh parsley, chopped
- Salt and ground black pepper, as required
- 1 (4-pound) bone-in, skin-on turkey breast
- 2 tablespoons olive oil

Directions:
1. In a bowl, add the butter, herbs, salt and black pepper and mix well.
2. Rub the herb mixture under skin evenly.
3. Coat the outside of turkey breast with oil.
4. Place the turkey breast into the greased baking pan.
5. Press "Power Button" of Ninja Foodi Digital Air Fry Oven and turn the dial to select the "Air Bake" mode.
6. Press the Time button and again turn the dial to set the cooking time to 40 minutes.
7. Now push the Temp button and rotate the dial to set the temperature at 350 degrees F.
8. Press "Start/Pause" button to start.
9. When the unit beeps to show that it is preheated, open the lid and insert baking pan in the oven.
10. Remove from oven and place the turkey breast onto a platter for about 5-10 minutes before slicing.
11. With a sharp knife, cut the turkey breast into desired sized slices and serve.

Nutrition Info: Calories 333 Total Fat 37 g Saturated Fat 12.4 g Cholesterol 209 mg Sodium 245 mg Total Carbs 1.8 g Fiber 1.1 g Sugar 0.1 g Protein 65.1 g

Seasoned Chicken Tenders

Servings: 2

Cooking Time: 10 Minutes

Ingredients:

- 8 ounces chicken tenders
- 1 teaspoon BBQ seasoning
- Salt and ground black pepper, as required

Directions:

1. Line the "Sheet Pan" with a lightly, greased piece of foil.
2. Set aside.
3. Season the chicken tenders with BBQ seasoning, salt and black pepper.
4. Arrange the chicken tenders onto the prepared "Sheet Pan" in a single layer.
5. Press "Power Button" of Ninja Foodi Digital Air Fry Oven and turn the dial to select the "Air Bake" mode.
6. Press the Time button and again turn the dial to set the cooking time to 10 minutes.
7. Now push the Temp button and rotate the dial to set the temperature at 450 degrees F.
8. Press "Start/Pause" button to start.
9. When the unit beeps to show that it is preheated, open the lid and insert "Sheet Pan" in the oven.
10. Serve hot.

Nutrition Info: Calories 220 Total Fat 8.4 g Saturated Fat 2.3 g Cholesterol 101 mg Sodium 315 mg Total Carbs 0.5 g Fiber 0 g Sugar 0 g Protein 32.8 g

Breaded Chicken Breast

Servings: 6
Cooking Time: 12 Minutes

Ingredients:

- 1 cup breadcrumbs
- ½ cup Parmesan cheese, grated
- ¼ cup fresh parsley, minced
- Salt and freshly ground black pepper, to taste
- 1½ pounds boneless, skinless chicken breasts
- 3 tablespoons olive oil
- Olive oil cooking spray

Directions:

1. In a shallow dish, add the breadcrumbs, Parmesan cheese, parsley, salt and black pepper mix well.
2. Rub the chicken breasts with oil and then, coat with the breadcrumbs mixture evenly.
3. Arrange the chicken breasts onto the sheet pan and spray with cooking spray.
4. Press "Power Button" of Ninja Foodi Digital Air Fry Oven and turn the dial to select "Air Fry" mode.
5. Press "Time Button" and again turn the dial to set the cooking time to 12 minutes.
6. Now push "Temp Button" and rotate the dial to set the temperature at 350 degrees F.
7. Press "Start/Pause" button to start.
8. When the unit beeps to show that it is preheated, open the lid and insert the sheet pan in the oven.
9. Flip the chicken breasts once halfway through.
10. When cooking time is complete, open the lid and transfer the chicken breasts onto a platter.
11. Serve hot.
12. Serving Suggestions: Enjoy these chicken breasts with honey mustard sauce.
13. Variation Tip: Pat dry the chicken breasts thoroughly before breading.

Nutrition Info: Calories: 371 Fat: 18g Sat Fat: 4.3g Carbohydrates: 13.1g Fiber: 0.9g Sugar: 1.1g Protein: 38g

Spiced Chicken Thighs

Servings: 4
Cooking Time: 20 Minutes
Ingredients:
- 1 teaspoon ground cumin
- 1 teaspoon garlic powder
- ½ teaspoon smoked paprika
- ½ teaspoon ground coriander
- Salt and ground black pepper, as required
- 4 (5-ounce) chicken thighs

Directions:
1. In a large bowl, add the spices, salt and black pepper and mix well.
2. Coat the chicken thighs with oil and then rub with spice mixture.
3. Arrange the chicken thighs onto the sheet pan.
4. Press "Power Button" of Ninja Foodi Digital Air Fry Oven and turn the dial to select "Air Fry" mode.
5. Press "Time Button" and again turn the dial to set the cooking time to 20 minutes.
6. Now push "Temp Button" and rotate the dial to set the temperature at 400 degrees F.
7. Press "Start/Pause" button to start.
8. When the unit beeps to show that it is preheated, open the lid and insert the sheet pan in the oven.
9. Flip the chicken thighs once halfway through.
10. When cooking time is complete, open the lid and transfer the chicken thighs onto serving plates.
11. Serve hot.
12. Serving Suggestions: Serve with a fresh green salad.
13. Variation Tip: Adjust the ratio of spices according to your spice tolerance.
Nutrition Info: Calories: 334 Fat: 17.7g Sat Fat: 3.9g Carbohydrates: 0.9g Fiber: 0.2g Sugar: 0.2g Protein: 41.3g

Hard-boiled Eggs

Servings: 6
Cooking Time: 16 Minutes
Ingredients:
- 6 eggs, large

Directions:
1. Keep the eggs on your air fryer's wire rack.
2. Set the temperature to 250.
3. Take out the eggs once they are done.
4. Place them in a bowl with ice water.
5. Peel them off and serve.
Nutrition Info: Calories 91, Carbohydrates 1g, Total Fat 7g, Protein 6g, Sugar 0g, Fiber 0g, Sodium 62mg

Herbed Turkey Breast

Servings: 6
Cooking Time: 40 Minutes

Ingredients:

- ¼ cup unsalted butter, softened
- 2 tablespoons fresh rosemary, chopped
- 2 tablespoon fresh thyme, chopped
- 2 tablespoons fresh sage, chopped
- 2 tablespoons fresh parsley, chopped
- Salt and freshly ground black pepper, to taste
- 1 (4-pound) bone-in, skin-on turkey breast
- 2 tablespoons olive oil

Directions:

1. In a bowl, add the butter, herbs, salt and black pepper and mix well.
2. Rub the herb mixture under skin evenly.
3. Coat the outside of turkey breast with oil.
4. Place the turkey breast into the greased baking pan.
5. Press "Power Button" of Ninja Foodi Digital Air Fry Oven and turn the dial to select "Air Bake" mode.
6. Press "Time Button" and again turn the dial to set the cooking time to 40 minutes.
7. Now push "Temp Button" and rotate the dial to set the temperature at 350 degrees F.
8. Press "Start/Pause" button to start.
9. When the unit beeps to show that it is preheated, open the lid and insert baking pan in the oven.
10. When cooking time is complete, open the lid and place the turkey breast onto a platter for about 5-10 minutes before slicing.
11. With a sharp knife, cut the turkey breast into desired sized slices and serve.
12. Serving Suggestions: Roasted potatoes will accompany this turkey breast nicely.
13. Variation Tip: Use unsalted butter.

Nutrition Info: Calories: 333 Fat: 37g Sat Fat: 12.4g Carbohydrates: 1.8g Fiber: 1.1g Sugar: 0.1g Protein: 65.1g

Air Fryer Chicken Wings

Servings: 4
Cooking Time: 30 Minutes

Ingredients:

- 1-1/2 oz. chicken wings
- 1 teaspoon garlic powder
- 1 teaspoon kosher salt
- 1 tablespoon of butter, unsalted and melted
- ½ cup hot sauce

Directions:

1. Keep your chicken wings in 1 layer. Use paper towels to pat them dry.
2. Sprinkle garlic powder and salt evenly.
3. Now keep these wings in your air fryer at 380°F.
4. Cook for 20 minutes. Toss after every 5 minutes. The wings should be cooked through and tender.
5. Bring up the temperature to 400 degrees F.
6. Cook for 5-8 minutes until it has turned golden brown and crispy.
7. Toss your wings with melted butter (optional) before serving.

Nutrition Info: Calories 291, Carbohydrates 1g, Total Fat 23g, Protein 20g, Sugar 0.3g, Fiber 0g, Sodium 593mg

Glazed Turkey Breast

Servings: 10
Cooking Time: 55 Minutes
Ingredients:
- 1 teaspoon dried thyme, crushed
- ½ teaspoon dried sage, crushed
- ½ teaspoon smoked paprika
- Salt and freshly ground black pepper, to taste
- 1 (5-pound) boneless turkey breast
- 2 teaspoons olive oil
- ¼ cup maple syrup
- 2 tablespoons Dijon mustard
- 1 tablespoon butter, softened

Directions:
1. In a bowl, mix together the herbs, paprika, salt, and black pepper.
2. Coat the turkey breast with oil evenly.
3. Now, coat the outer side of turkey breast with herb mixture.
4. Press "Power Button" of Ninja Foodi Digital Air Fry Oven and turn the dial to select "Air Fry" mode.
5. Press "Time Button" and again turn the dial to set the cooking time to 55 minutes.
6. Now push "Temp Button" and rotate the dial to set the temperature at 350 degrees F.
7. Press "Start/Pause" button to start.
8. When the unit beeps to show that it is preheated, open the lid and grease the air fry basket.
9. Arrange the turkey breast into the prepared basket and insert in the oven.
10. While cooking, flip the turkey breast once after 25 minutes and then after 37 minutes.
11. Meanwhile, in a bowl, mix together the maple syrup, mustard, and butter.
12. After 50 minutes of cooking, press "Start/Pause" to pause cooking.
13. Remove the basket from Air Fryer and coat the turkey breast with glaze evenly.
14. Again, insert the basket in the oven and press "Start/Pause" to resume cooking.
15. When cooking time is complete, open the lid and place the turkey breast onto a cutting board for about 10 minutes before slicing.
16. With a sharp knife, cut the turkey breast into desired sized slices and serve.
17. Serving Suggestions: Green bean and goats cheese salad will be best for turkey meat.
18. Variation Tip: Place the turkey into the basket with the breast side down.
Nutrition Info: Calories: 30w, Fat: 3.3g, Sat Fat: 0.9g, Carbohydrates: 5.6g, Fiber: 0.2g Sugar: 4.7g, Protein: 26.2g

Turkey Breasts

Servings: 6
Cooking Time: 40 Minutes

Ingredients:

- 2-3/4 oz. turkey breasts, with skin
- 1 tablespoon rosemary, chopped
- 1 teaspoon chive, chopped
- 2 tablespoons of butter, unsalted
- 1 teaspoon garlic, minced

Directions:

1. Preheat your air fryer to 175 degrees C or 350 degrees F.
2. Keep the chives, rosemary, garlic, pepper, and salt on your cutting board.
3. Make thin slices of butter and place on the seasonings and herbs. Blend well.
4. Pat the herbed butter on both sides of the turkey breasts.
5. Keep the turkey in the air fryer basket, skin-down side.
6. Fry for 17 minutes.
7. Turn the skin-side up and keep frying for 8 more minutes at 74 degrees C or 165 degrees F.
8. Transfer to a plate. Set aside for 10 minutes.
9. Slice before serving.

Nutrition Info: Calories 287, Carbohydrates 0.3g, Cholesterol 86mg, Total Fat 14g, Protein 40g, Sugar 0g, Fiber 0.1g, Sodium 913mg

MEAT RECIPES

Mushrooms With Steak

Servings: 4
Cooking Time: 10 Minutes
Ingredients:
- 1 oz. sirloin beef steak, cut into small 1-inch cubes
- ¼ cup Worcestershire sauce
- 8 oz. sliced button mushrooms
- 1 tablespoon of olive oil
- 1 teaspoon chili flakes, crushed

Directions:
1. Combine the mushrooms, steak, olive oil Worcestershire sauce, and chili flakes in your bowl.
2. Keep it refrigerated for 4 hours minimum.
3. Take out 30 minutes before cooking.
4. Preheat your oven to 200 degrees C or 400 degrees F.
5. Drain out the marinade from your steak mixture.
6. Now keep the mushrooms and steak in the air fryer basket.
7. Cook for 5 minutes in the air fryer.
8. Toss and then cook for another 5 minutes.
9. Transfer the mushrooms and steak to a serving plate.

Nutrition Info: Calories 261, Carbohydrates 6g, Cholesterol 60mg, Total Fat 17g, Protein 21g, Sugar 3g, Fiber 0.9g, Sodium 213mg

Buttered Rib Eye Steak

Servings: 3
Cooking Time: 14 Minutes
Ingredients:
- 2 (8-ounce) rib eye steaks
- 2 tablespoons butter, melted
- Salt and ground black pepper, as required

Directions:
1. Coat the steak with butter and then, sprinkle with salt and black pepper evenly.
2. Press "Power Button" of Ninja Foodi Digital Air Fry Oven and turn the dial to select the "Air Roast" mode.
3. Press the Time button and again turn the dial to set the cooking time to 14 minutes.
4. Now push the Temp button and rotate the dial to set the temperature at 400 degrees F.
5. Press "Start/Pause" button to start.
6. When the unit beeps to show that it is preheated, open the lid and grease "Air Fry Basket".
7. Arrange the steaks into "Air Fry Basket" and insert in the oven.
8. Remove from the oven and place steaks onto a platter for about 5 minutes.
9. Cut each steak into desired size slices and serve.

Nutrition Info: Calories 388 Total Fat 23.7 g Saturated Fat 110.2 g Cholesterol 154 mg Sodium 278 mg Total Carbs 0 g Fiber 0 g Sugar 0 g Protein 41 g

Glazed Lamb Chops

Servings: 4
Cooking Time: 15 Minutes
Ingredients:
- 1 tablespoon Dijon mustard
- ½ tablespoon fresh lime juice
- 1 teaspoon honey
- ½ teaspoon olive oil
- Salt and freshly ground black pepper, to taste
- 4 (4-ounce) lamb loin chops

Directions:
1. In a black pepper large bowl, mix together the mustard, lemon juice, oil, honey, salt, and black pepper.
2. Add the chops and coat with the mixture generously.
3. Place the chops onto the greased sheet pan.
4. Press "Power Button" of Ninja Foodi Digital Air Fry Oven and turn the dial to select "Air Bake" mode.
5. Press "Time Button" and again turn the dial to set the cooking time to 15 minutes.
6. Now push "Temp Button" and rotate the dial to set the temperature at 390 degrees F.
7. Press "Start/Pause" button to start.
8. When the unit beeps to show that it is preheated, open the lid and insert the sheet pan in the oven.
9. Flip the chops once halfway through.
10. When cooking time is complete, open the lid and transfer the chops onto serving plates.
11. Serve hot.
12. Serving Suggestions: Serve the chops with mashed potatoes or polenta.
13. Variation Tip: Remember to pat dry the chops before seasoning.
Nutrition Info: Calories: 224 Fat: 9.1g Sat Fat: 3.1g Carbohydrates: 1.7g Fiber: 0.1g Sugar: 1.5g Protein: 32g

Herbed Pork Chops

Servings: 3
Cooking Time: 12 Minutes

Ingredients:

- 2 garlic cloves, minced
- ½ tablespoons fresh cilantro, chopped
- ½ tablespoons fresh rosemary, chopped
- ½ tablespoons fresh parsley, chopped
- 2 tablespoons olive oil
- ¾ tablespoons Dijon mustard
- 1 tablespoon ground coriander
- 1 teaspoon sugar
- Salt, to taste
- 3 (6-ounce) (1-inch thick) pork chops

Directions:

1. In a bowl, mix together the garlic, herbs, oil, mustard, coriander, sugar, and salt.
2. Add the pork chops and coat with marinade generously.
3. Cover the bowl and refrigerate for about 2-3 hours.
4. Remove chops from the refrigerator and set aside at room temperature for about 30 minutes.
5. Press "Power Button" of Ninja Foodi Digital Air Fry Oven and turn the dial to select "Air Fry" mode.
6. Press "Time Button" and again turn the dial to set the cooking time to 12 minutes.
7. Now push "Temp Button" and rotate the dial to set the temperature at 390 degrees F.
8. Press "Start/Pause" button to start.
9. When the unit beeps to show that it is preheated, open the lid and grease the air fry basket.
10. Arrange chops into the prepared Air Fryer basket in a single layer and insert in the oven.
11. When cooking time is complete, open the lid and transfer the chops onto plates.
12. Serve hot.
13. Serving Suggestions: Serve thee chops with curried potato salad.
14. Variation Tip: Bring the pork chops to room temperature before cooking.

Nutrition Info: Calories: 341 Fat: 25.5g Sat Fat: 6.8g Carbohydrates: 2.9g Fiber: 0.4g Sugar: 1.4g Protein: 32.3g

Buttered Leg Of Lamb

Servings: 8
Cooking Time: 1¼ Hours
Ingredients:

- 1 (2¼-pound) boneless leg of lamb
- 3 tablespoons butter, melted
- Salt and freshly ground black pepper, to taste
- 4 fresh rosemary sprigs

Directions:

1. Rub the leg of lamb with butter and sprinkle with salt and black pepper.
2. Wrap the leg of lamb with rosemary sprigs.
3. Press "Power Button" of Ninja Foodi Digital Air Fry Oven and turn the dial to select "Air Fry" mode.
4. Press "Time Button" and again turn the dial to set the cooking time to 75 minutes.
5. Now push "Temp Button" and rotate the dial to set the temperature at 300 degrees F.
6. Press "Start/Pause" button to start.
7. When the unit beeps to show that it is preheated, open the lid and grease air fry basket.
8. Arrange the leg of lamb into the air fry basket and insert in the oven.
9. When cooking time is complete, open the lid and place the leg of lamb onto a cutting board for about 10 minutes before slicing.
10. Cut into desired sized pieces and serve.
11. Serving Suggestions: Dijon mustard glazed carrots will be great if served with le
12. Variation Tip: You can add spices of your choice for seasoning of the leg of lamb.

Nutrition Info: Calories: 278 Fat: 13.8g Sat Fat: 6.1g Carbohydrates: 0.5g Fiber: 0.4g Sugar: 0g Protein: 35.9g

Beef Kabobs

Servings: 4
Cooking Time: 10 Minutes
Ingredients:

- 1 oz. beef ribs, cut into small 1-inch pieces
- 2 tablespoons soy sauce
- 1/3 cup low-fat sour cream
- 1 bell pepper
- ½ onion

Directions:

1. Mix soy sauce and sour cream in a bowl.
2. Keep the chunks of beef in the bowl. Marinate for 30 minutes' minimum.
3. Now cut the onion and bell pepper into one-inch pieces.
4. Soak 8 skewers in water.
5. Thread the bell pepper, onions, and beef on the skewers. Add some pepper.
6. Cook for 10 minutes in your pre-heated air fryer. Turn after 5 minutes.

Nutrition Info: Calories 297, Carbohydrates 4g, Cholesterol 84mg, Total Fat 21g, Protein 23g, Sugar 2g, Sodium 609mg, Calcium 49mg

Pork Meatloaf

Servings: 8
Cooking Time: 1 Hour 5 Minutes

Ingredients:

- For Meatloaf:
- 2 pounds lean ground pork
- 1 cup quick-cooking oats
- ½ cup carrot, peeled and shredded
- 1 medium onion, chopped
- ½ cup fat-free milk
- ¼ of egg, beaten
- 2 tablespoons ketchup
- 1 teaspoon garlic powder
- ¼ teaspoon ground black pepper
- For Topping:
- ¼ cup ketchup
- ¼ cup quick-cooking oats

Directions:

1. For meatloaf: in a bowl, add all the ingredients and mix until well combined.
2. For topping: in another bowl, add all the ingredients and mix until well combined.
3. Transfer the mixture into a greased loaf pan and top with the topping mixture.
4. Press "Power Button" of Ninja Foodi Digital Air Fry Oven and turn the dial to select "Air Bake" mode.
5. Press "Time Button" and again turn the dial to set the cooking time to 65 minutes.
6. Now push "Temp Button" and rotate the dial to set the temperature at 350 degrees F.
7. Press "Start/Pause" button to start.
8. When the unit beeps to show that it is preheated, open the lid.
9. Arrange the loaf pan over the wire rack and insert in the oven.
10. When cooking time is complete, open the lid and place the loaf pan onto a wire rack for about 10 minutes.
11. Carefully invert the loaf onto the wire rack.
12. Cut into desired sized slices and serve.
13. Serving Suggestions: Baked cauliflower will nicely accompany this meatloaf.
14. Variation Tip: Add in a sprinkling of Italian seasoning in meatloaf.

Nutrition Info: Calories: 239 Fat: 9.1g Sat Fat: 2.7g Carbohydrates: 14.5g Fiber: 1.8g Sugar: 4.5g Protein: 25.1g

Sweet Potato, Brown Rice, And Lamb

Servings: 2
Cooking Time: 10 Minutes
Ingredients:
- ¼ cup lamb, cooked and puréed
- ½ cup cooked brown rice
- ¼ cup of sweet potato purée

Directions:
1. Keep all the ingredients in your bowl.
2. Pulse until you achieve the desired consistency.
3. Process with milk to get a smoother consistency.
4. Store in an airtight container. Refrigerate.

Nutrition Info: Calories 37, Carbohydrates 5g, Cholesterol 7mg, Total Fat 1g, Protein 2g, Fiber 1g, Sodium 6mg

Spiced Pork Shoulder

Servings: 6
Cooking Time: 55 Minutes
Ingredients:
- 1 teaspoon ground cumin
- 1 teaspoon cayenne pepper
- ½ teaspoon garlic powder
- ½ teaspoon onion powder
- Salt and ground black pepper, as required
- 2 pounds skin-on pork shoulder

Directions:
1. In a small bowl, place the spices, salt and black pepper and mix well.
2. Arrange the pork shoulder onto a cutting board, skin-side down.
3. Season the inner side of pork shoulder with salt and black pepper.
4. With kitchen twines, tie the pork shoulder into a long round cylinder shape.
5. Season the outer side of pork shoulder with spice mixture.
6. Press "Power Button" of Ninja Foodi Digital Air Fry Oven and turn the dial to select the "Air Roast" mode.
7. Press the Time button and again turn the dial to set the cooking time to 55 minutes.
8. Now push the Temp button and rotate the dial to set the temperature at 350 degrees F.
9. Press "Start/Pause" button to start.
10. When the unit beeps to show that it is preheated, open the lid and grease "Air Fry Basket".
11. Arrange the pork shoulder into "Air Fry Basket" and insert in the oven.
12. Remove from oven and place the pork shoulder onto a platter for about 10 minutes before slicing.
13. With a sharp knife, cut the pork shoulder into desired sized slices and serve.

Nutrition Info: Calories 445 Total Fat 32.5 g Saturated Fat 11.9 g Cholesterol 136 mg Sodium 131 mg Total Carbs 0.7 g Fiber 0.2 g Sugar 0.2 g Protein 35.4 g

Spiced Flank Steak

Servings: 6
Cooking Time: 12 Minutes

Ingredients:
- 2 tablespoons balsamic vinegar
- 2 tablespoons olive oil
- 3 garlic cloves, minced
- 1 teaspoon red chili powder
- 1 teaspoon ground cumin
- 1 teaspoon onion powder
- Salt and freshly ground black pepper, to taste
- 1 (2-pound) flank steak

Directions:
1. In a large bowl, mix together the vinegar, spices, salt and black pepper.
2. Add the steak and coat with mixture generously.
3. Cover the bowl and place in the refrigerator for at least 1 hour.
4. Remove the steak from bowl and place onto the greased sheet pan.
5. Press "Power Button" of Ninja Foodi Digital Air Fry Oven and turn the dial to select the "Air Broil" mode.
6. Press "Time Button" and again turn the dial to set the cooking time to 12 minutes.
7. Press "Start/Pause" button to start.
8. When the unit beeps to show that it is preheated, open the lid and insert the sheet pan in the oven.
9. Flip the steak once halfway through.
10. When cooking time is complete, open the lid and place the steak onto a cutting board.
11. With a sharp knife, cut the steak into desired sized slices and serve.
12. Serving Suggestions: Enjoy this steak with a drizzling of fresh lemon juice.
13. Variation Tip: choose the steak that is as uniform in thickness.

Nutrition Info: Calories: 341 Fat: 17.4g Sat Fat: 5.9g Carbohydrates: 1.3g Fiber: 0.2g Sugar: 0.2g Protein: 42.3g

Roast Beef

Servings: 6

Cooking Time: 45 Minutes

Ingredients:

- 2 oz. beef roast
- 1 tablespoon olive oil
- 2 teaspoon thyme and rosemary
- 1 teaspoon of salt
- 1 onion, medium

Directions:

1. Preheat your air fryer to 200 degrees C or 390 degrees F.
2. Mix the rosemary, oil, and salt on a plate.
3. Use paper towels to pat dry your beef roast.
4. Keep it on a plate. Coat the oil-herb mix on the outside.
5. Keep your beef roast in the air fryer basket.
6. Peel the onion. Cut it in half. Keep the halves next to your roast.
7. Cook for 12 minutes.
8. Change the temperature to 180 degrees C or 360 degrees F.
9. Cook for another 25 minutes.
10. Take it out and cover using kitchen foil.
11. Let it rest for 5 minutes.
12. Carve it thinly against the grain.
13. Serve with steamed or roasted vegetables, gravy, and wholegrain mustard.

Nutrition Info: Calories 221, Carbohydrates 2g, Cholesterol 83mg, Total Fat 9g, Protein 33g, Fiber 1g, Sugar 1g, Sodium 282mg

Italian-style Meatballs

Servings: 12

Cooking Time: 35 Minutes

Ingredients:

- 10 oz. lean beef, ground
- 3 garlic cloves, minced
- 5 oz. turkey sausage
- 2 tablespoons shallot, minced
- 1 large egg, lightly beaten
- 2 tablespoons of olive oil
- 1 tablespoon of rosemary and thyme, chopped

Directions:

1. Preheat your air fryer to 400 degrees F.
2. Heat oil and add the shallot. Cook for 1-2 minutes.
3. Add the garlic now and cook. Take out from the heat.
4. Add the garlic and cooked shallot along with the egg, turkey sausage, beef, rosemary, thyme, and salt. Combine well by stirring.
5. Shape the mixture gently into 1-1/2 inch small balls.
6. Keep the balls in your air fryer basket.
7. Cook your meatballs at 400 degrees F. They should turn light brown.
8. Take out. Keep warm.
9. Serve the meatballs over rice or pasta.

Nutrition Info: Calories 175, Carbohydrates 0g, Total Fat 15g, Fiber 0g, Protein 10g, Sugar 0g, Sodium 254mg

Simple Beef Tenderloin

Servings: 10
Cooking Time: 50 Minutes

Ingredients:

- 1 (3½-pound) beef tenderloin, trimmed
- 2 tablespoons olive oil
- Salt and ground black pepper, as required

Directions:

1. With kitchen twine, tie the tenderloin.
2. Rub the tenderloin with oil and season with salt and black pepper.
3. Place the tenderloin into the greased baking pan.
4. Press "Power Button" of Ninja Foodi Digital Air Fry Oven and turn the dial to select the "Air Roast" mode.
5. Press the Time button and again turn the dial to set the cooking time to 50 minutes.
6. Now push the Temp button and rotate the dial to set the temperature at 400 degrees F.
7. Press "Start/Pause" button to start.
8. When the unit beeps to show that it is preheated, open the lid and insert baking pan in the oven.
9. Remove from oven and place the tenderloin onto a platter for about 10 minutes before slicing.
10. With a sharp knife, cut the tenderloin into desired sized slices and serve.

Nutrition Info: Calories 351 Total Fat 17.3 g Saturated Fat 5.9 g Cholesterol 146 mg Sodium 109 mg Total Carbs 0 g Fiber 0 g Sugar 0 g Protein 46 g

Glazed Pork Tenderloin

Servings: 3
Cooking Time: 20 Minutes

Ingredients:

- 2 tablespoons Sriracha
- 2 tablespoons maple syrup
- ¼ teaspoon red pepper flakes, crushed
- Salt, to taste
- 1 pound pork tenderloin

Directions:

1. In a small bowl, add the Sriracha, maple syrup, red pepper flakes and salt and mix well.
2. Brush the pork tenderloin with mixture evenly.
3. Press "Power Button" of Ninja Foodi Digital Air Fry Oven and turn the dial to select "Air Fry" mode.
4. Press "Time Button" and again turn the dial to set the cooking time to 20 minutes.
5. Now push "Temp Button" and rotate the dial to set the temperature at 350 degrees F.
6. Press "Start/Pause" button to start.
7. When the unit beeps to show that it is preheated, open the lid and grease air fry basket.
8. Arrange the pork tenderloin into the air fry basket and insert in the oven.
9. When cooking time is complete, open the lid and place the pork tenderloin onto a platter for about 10 minutes before slicing.
10. With a sharp knife, cut the roast into desired sized slices and serve.
11. Serving Suggestions: Fig and arugula salad will brighten the taste of tenderloin.
12. Variation Tip: The addition of dried herbs will add a delish touch in pork tenderloin.

Nutrition Info: Calories: 261 Fat: 5.4g Sat Fat: 1.8g Carbohydrates: 11g Fiber: 0g Sugar: 8g Protein: 39.6g

Glazed Lamb Meatballs

Servings: 8
Cooking Time: 30 Minutes
Ingredients:
- For Meatballs:
- 2 pounds lean ground lamb
- 2/3 cup quick-cooking oats
- ½ cup Ritz crackers, crushed
- 1 (5-ounce) can evaporated milk
- 2 large eggs, beaten lightly
- 1 teaspoon maple syrup
- 1 tablespoon dried onion, minced
- Salt and freshly ground black pepper, to taste
- For Sauce:
- 1/3 cup orange marmalade
- 1/3 cup maple syrup
- 1/3 cup sugar
- 2 tablespoons cornstarch
- 2 tablespoons soy sauce
- 1-2 tablespoons Sriracha
- 1 tablespoon Worcestershire sauce

Directions:
1. For meatballs: in a large bowl, add all the ingredients and mix until well combined.
2. Make 1½-inch balls from the mixture.
3. Arrange half of the meatballs onto the greased sheet pan in a single layer.
4. Press "Power Button" of Ninja Foodi Digital Air Fry Oven and turn the dial to select "Air Fry" mode.
5. Press "Time Button" and again turn the dial to set the cooking time to 15 minutes.
6. Now push "Temp Button" and rotate the dial to set the temperature at 380 degrees F.
7. Press "Start/Pause" button to start.
8. When the unit beeps to show that it is preheated, open the lid and insert the sheet pan in the oven.
9. Flip the meatballs once halfway through.
10. When cooking time is complete, open the lid and transfer the meatballs into a bowl.
11. Repeat with the remaining meatballs.
12. Meanwhile, for sauce: in a small pan, add all the ingredients over medium heat and cook until thickened, stirring continuously.
13. Serve the meatballs with the topping of sauce.
14. Serving Suggestions: Mashed buttery potatoes make a classic pairing with meatballs.
15. Variation Tip: You can adjust the ratio of sweetener according to your taste.
Nutrition Info: Calories: 413, Fat: 11.9g, Sat Fat: 4.3g Carbohydrates: 39.5g, Fiber: 1g Sugar: 28.2g, Protein: 36.2g

Pork Skewers With Mango Salsa & Black Bean

Servings: 4

Cooking Time: 10 Minutes

Ingredients:

- 1 lb. pork tenderloin, cut into small cubes
- ½ can black beans, rinsed and drained
- 1 mango, peeled, seeded, and chopped
- 4-1/2 teaspoons of onion powder
- 4-1/2 teaspoons thyme, crushed
- 1 tablespoon vegetable oil
- ¼ teaspoon cloves, ground

Directions:

1. Stir in the thyme, onion powder, salt, and cloves in a bowl to create the seasoning mixture.
2. Keep a tablespoon of this for the pork. Transfer the remaining to an airtight container for later.
3. Preheat your air fryer to 175 degrees C or 350 degrees F.
4. Thread the chunks of pork into the skewers.
5. Brush oil on the pork. Sprinkle the seasoning mix on all sides.
6. Keep in your air fryer basket.
7. Cook for 5 minutes.
8. Mash one-third of the mango in your bowl in the meantime.
9. Stir the remaining mango in, and also salt, pepper, and black beans.
10. Serve the salsa with the pork skewers.

Nutrition Info: Calories 372, Carbohydrates 35g, Cholesterol 49mg, Total Fat 16g, Fiber 7g, Protein 22g, Sugar 18g, Sodium 1268mg

Rosemary Garlic Lamb Chops

Servings: 2
Cooking Time: 12 Minutes
Ingredients:
- 4 chops of lamb
- 1 teaspoon olive oil
- 2 teaspoon garlic puree
- Fresh garlic
- Fresh rosemary

Directions:
1. Keep your lamb chops in the fryer grill pan.
2. Season the chops with pepper and salt. Brush some olive oil.
3. Add some garlic puree on each chop.
4. Cover the grill pan gaps with garlic cloves and rosemary sprigs.
5. Refrigerate the grill pan to marinate.
6. Take out after 1 hour. Keep in the fryer and cook for 5 minutes.
7. Use your spatula to turn the chops over.
8. Add some olive oil and cook for another 5 minutes.
9. Set aside for a minute.
10. Take out the rosemary and garlic before serving.

Nutrition Info: Calories 678, Carbohydrates 1g, Cholesterol 257mg, Total Fat 38g, Protein 83g, Sugar 0g, Sodium 200mg

Seasoned Sirloin Steak

Servings: 2
Cooking Time: 12 Minutes
Ingredients:
- 2 (7-ounce) top sirloin steak
- 1 tablespoon steak seasoning
- Salt and ground black pepper, as required

Directions:
1. Season each steak with steak seasoning, salt and black pepper.
2. Arrange the steaks onto the greased cooking pan.
3. Press "Power Button" of Ninja Foodi Digital Air Fry Oven and turn the dial to select the "Air Fry" mode.
4. Press the Time button and again turn the dial to set the cooking time to 12 minutes.
5. Now push the Temp button and rotate the dial to set the temperature at 400 degrees F.
6. Press "Start/Pause" button to start.
7. When the unit beeps to show that it is preheated, open the lid and insert baking pan in the oven.
8. Flip the steaks once halfway through.
9. Remove from oven and serve.

Nutrition Info: Calories 369 Total Fat 12.4 g Saturated Fat 4.7 g Cholesterol 177 mg Sodium 208 mg Total Carbs 0 g Fiber 0 g Sugar 0 g Protein 60.2 g

Ranch Pork Chops

Servings: 4

Cooking Time: 15 Minutes

Ingredients:

- 4 pork chops, boneless and center-cut
- 2 teaspoons salad dressing mix

Directions:

1. Keep your pork chops on a plate.
2. Apply cooking spray on both sides lightly.
3. Sprinkle the seasoning mixture on both sides.
4. Allow to sit at room temperature for 5 minutes.
5. Apply cooking spray on the basket.
6. Preheat your air fryer to 200 degrees C or 390 degrees F.
7. Keep the chops in the air fryer. It shouldn't get overcrowded.
8. Cook for 5 minutes. Now flip your chops and cook for another 5 minutes.
9. Allow it to rest before serving.

Nutrition Info: Calories 276, Carbohydrates 1g, Cholesterol 107mg, Total Fat 12g, Fiber 0g, Protein 41g, Sugar 0g, Sodium 148mg

Pork Stuffed Bell Peppers

Servings: 4
Cooking Time: 1 Hour 10 Minutes

Ingredients:

- 4 medium green bell peppers
- 2/3-pound ground pork
- 2 cups cooked white rice
- 1½ cups marinara sauce, divided
- 1 teaspoon Worcestershire sauce
- 1 teaspoon Italian seasoning
- Salt and ground black pepper, as required
- ½ cup mozzarella cheese, shredded

Directions:

1. Cut the tops from bell peppers and then carefully remove the seeds.
2. Heat a large skillet over medium heat and cook the pork for bout 6-8 minutes, breaking into crumbles.
3. Add the rice, ¾ cup of marinara sauce, Worcestershire sauce, Italian seasoning, salt and black pepper and stir to combine.
4. Remove from the heat.
5. Arrange the bell peppers into the greased baking pan.
6. Carefully, stuff each bell pepper with the pork mixture and top each with the remaining sauce.
7. Press "Power Button" of Ninja Foodi Digital Air Fry Oven and turn the dial to select the "Air Bake" mode.
8. Press the Time button and again turn the dial to set the cooking time to 60 minutes.
9. Now push the Temp button and rotate the dial to set the temperature at 350 degrees F.
10. Press "Start/Pause" button to start.
11. When the unit beeps to show that it is preheated, open the lid.
12. Insert the baking pan in oven.
13. After 50 minutes of cooking, top each bell pepper with cheese.
14. Serve warm.

Nutrition Info: Calories 580 Total Fat 7.1 g Saturated Fat 2.2 g Cholesterol 60 mg Sodium 509 mg Total Carbs 96.4 g Fiber 5.2 g Sugar 14.8 g Protein 30.3 g

Buttered Rib-eye Steak

Servings: 3
Cooking Time: 14 Minutes

Ingredients:

- 2 (8-ounce) rib-eye steaks
- 2 tablespoons butter, melted
- Salt and freshly ground black pepper, to taste

Directions:

1. Coat the steak with butter and then sprinkle with salt and black pepper evenly.
2. Press "Power Button" of Ninja Foodi Digital Air Fry Oven and turn the dial to select "Air Roast" mode.
3. Press "Time Button" and again turn the dial to set the cooking time to 14 minutes.
4. Now push "Temp Button" and rotate the dial to set the temperature at 400 degrees F.
5. Press "Start/Pause" button to start.
6. When the unit beeps to show that it is preheated, open the lid and grease the air fry basket.
7. Arrange the steaks into the air fry basket and insert in the oven.
8. When cooking time is complete, open the lid and place steaks onto a platter for about 5 minutes.
9. Cut each steak into desired sized slices and serve.
10. Serving Suggestions: Enjoy this steak with grille potatoes.
11. Variation Tip: Rib-eye steak is best when it's cooked medium-rare.

Nutrition Info: Calories: 383 Fat: 23.7g Sat Fat: 10.2g Carbohydrates: 0g Fiber: 0g Sugar: 0g Protein: 41g

VEGETARIAN AND VEGAN RECIPES

Parmesan Asparagus

Servings: 3
Cooking Time: 10 Minutes
Ingredients:
- 1 pound fresh asparagus, trimmed
- 1 tablespoon Parmesan cheese, grated
- 1 tablespoon butter, melted
- 1 teaspoon garlic powder
- Salt and freshly ground black pepper, to taste

Directions:
1. In a bowl, mix together the asparagus, cheese, butter, garlic powder, salt, and black pepper.
2. Press "Power Button" of Ninja Foodi Digital Air Fry Oven and turn the dial to select "Air Fry" mode.
3. Press "Time Button" and again turn the dial to set the cooking time to 10 minutes.
4. Now push "Temp Button" and rotate the dial to set the temperature at 400 degrees F.
5. Press "Start/Pause" button to start.
6. When the unit beeps to show that it is preheated, open the lid and grease the air fry basket.
7. Arrange the veggie mixture into the prepared air fry basket and insert in the oven.
8. When cooking time is complete, open the lid and transfer the asparagus onto serving plates.
9. Serve hot.
10. Serving Suggestions: Serve with the garnishing of pine nuts.
11. Variation Tip: you can use fresh garlic instead of garlic powder.

Nutrition Info: Calories: 73 Fat: 4.4g Sat Fat: 2.7g Carbohydrates: 6.6g Fiber: 3.3g Sugar: 3.1g Protein: 4.2g

Garlicky Brussels Sprout

Servings: 4
Cooking Time: 15 Minutes

Ingredients:

- 1 pound Brussels sprouts, cut in half
- 2 tablespoons oil
- 2 garlic cloves, minced
- ¼ teaspoon red pepper flakes, crushed
- Salt and freshly ground black pepper, to taste

Directions:

1. In a bowl, add all the ingredients and toss to coat well.
2. Press "Power Button" of Ninja Foodi Digital Air Fry Oven and turn the dial to select "Air Fry" mode.
3. Press "Time Button" and again turn the dial to set the cooking time to 12 minutes.
4. Now push "Temp Button" and rotate the dial to set the temperature at 390 degrees F.
5. Press "Start/Pause" button to start.
6. When the unit beeps to show that it is preheated, open the lid.
7. Arrange the Brussels sprouts into the air fry basket and insert in the oven.
8. When cooking time is complete, open the lid and transfer the Brussels sprouts onto serving plates.
9. Serve hot.
10. Serving Suggestions: Sprinkle with flaky sea salt before serving.
11. Variation Tip: Look for small to medium sprouts for better taste.

Nutrition Info: Calories: 113 Fat: 9g Sat Fat: 1.3g Carbohydrates: 8.3g Fiber: 2.6g Sugar: 4.2g Protein: 2.8g

Potato Gratin

Servings: 4
Cooking Time: 20 Minutes
Ingredients:
- 2 large potatoes, sliced thinly
- 5½ tablespoons cream
- 2 eggs
- 1 tablespoon plain flour
- ½ cup cheddar cheese, grated

Directions:
1. Press "Power Button" of Ninja Foodi Digital Air Fry Oven and turn the dial to select "Air Fry" mode.
2. Press "Time Button" and again turn the dial to set the cooking time to 10 minutes.
3. Now push "Temp Button" and rotate the dial to set the temperature at 355 degrees F.
4. Press "Start/Pause" button to start.
5. When the unit beeps to show that it is preheated, open the lid.
6. Arrange the potato slices in the air fry basket and insert in the oven.
7. Meanwhile, in a bowl, add cream, eggs and flour and mix until a thick sauce forms.
8. When cooking time is complete, open the lid and remove the potato slices from the basket.
9. Divide the potato slices in 4 ramekins evenly and top with the egg mixture evenly, followed by the cheese.
10. Press "Power Button" of Ninja Foodi Digital Air Fry Oven and turn the dial to select "Air Fry" mode.
11. Press "Time Button" and again turn the dial to set the cooking time to 10 minutes.
12. Now push "Temp Button" and rotate the dial to set the temperature at 390 degrees F.
13. Arrange the ramekins in the air fry basket and insert in the oven.
14. Press "Start/Pause" button to start.
15. When cooking time is complete, open the lid and remove the ramekins from the oven.
16. Serve warm.
17. Serving Suggestions: Serve this gratin with fresh lettuce.
18. Variation Tip: Make sure to cut the potato slices thinly.
Nutrition Info: Calories: 233 Fat: 8g Sat Fat: 4.3g Carbohydrates: 31.3g Fiber: 4.5g Sugar: 2.7g Protein: 9.7g

Cheesy Kale

Servings: 3
Cooking Time: 15 Minutes
Ingredients:
- 1-pound fresh kale, tough ribs removed and chopped
- 3 tablespoons olive oil
- Salt and ground black pepper, as required
- 1 cup goat cheese, crumbled
- 1 teaspoon fresh lemon juice

Directions:
1. In a bowl, add the kale, oil, salt and black pepper and mix well.
2. Press "Power Button" of Ninja Foodi Digital Air Fry Oven and turn the dial to select the "Air Fry" mode.
3. Press the Time button and again turn the dial to set the cooking time to 15 minutes.
4. Now push the Temp button and rotate the dial to set the temperature at 340 degrees F.
5. Press "Start/Pause" button to start.
6. When the unit beeps to show that it is preheated, open the lid and grease "Air Fry Basket".
7. Arrange the kale into "Air Fry Basket" and insert in the oven.
8. Remove from oven and immediately, transfer the kale mixture into a bowl.
9. Stir in the cheese and lemon juice and serve hot.

Nutrition Info: Calories 327 Total Fat 24.7 g Saturated Fat 9.5 g Cholesterol 45 mg Sodium 674 mg Total Carbs 17.9 g Fiber 2.3 g Sugar 2.1 g Protein 11.6 g

Baked Potatoes

Servings: 2
Cooking Time: 1 Hour
Ingredients:
- 1 tablespoon peanut oil
- 2 large potatoes, scrubbed
- ½ teaspoon of coarse sea salt

Directions:
1. Preheat your air fryer to 200 degrees C or 400 degrees F.
2. Brush peanut oil on your potatoes.
3. Sprinkle some salt.
4. Keep them in the basket of your air fryer.
5. Cook the potatoes for an hour.

Nutrition Info: Calories 360, Carbohydrates 64g, Cholesterol 0mg, Total Fat 8g, Protein 8g, Sugar 3g, Fiber 8g, Sodium 462mg

Air-fried Italian-style Ratatouille

Servings: 4

Cooking Time: 25 Minutes

Ingredients:

- ½ eggplant, cubed into small pieces
- 1 medium-sized tomato, cubed
- 1 zucchini, cubed
- 2 oregano sprigs, stemmed and chopped
- 1 tablespoon olive oil
- 1 tablespoon of white wine

Directions:

1. Preheat your air fryer to 200 degrees C or 400 degrees F.
2. Place the zucchini, eggplant, and tomato in a bowl.
3. Now add the oregano, pepper, and salt.
4. Distribute well by mixing.
5. Drizzle in the white wine and oil. Coat the vegetables well.
6. Pour the vegetable mix into your baking dish.
7. Insert this into your air fryer basket.
8. Cook for 15 minutes, stirring once.
9. Stir once more and keep cooking until it gets tender.
10. Turn the air fryer off.
11. Let it rest for 5-7 minutes before serving.

Nutrition Info: Calories 93, Carbohydrates 10g, Cholesterol 0mg, Total Fat 5g, Protein 2g, Sugar 5g, Fiber 3g, Sodium 48mg

Fried Chickpeas

Servings: 4

Cooking Time: 20 Minutes

Ingredients:

- 1 can chickpeas, rinsed and drained
- 1 tablespoon olive oil
- 1 tablespoon of nutritional yeast
- 1 teaspoon garlic, granulated
- 1 teaspoon of smoked paprika

Directions:

1. Spread the chickpeas on paper towels. Cover using a second paper towel later.
2. Allow them to dry for half an hour.
3. Preheat your air fryer to 180 degrees C or 355 degrees F.
4. Bring together the nutritional yeast, chickpeas, smoked paprika, olive oil, salt, and garlic in a mid-sized bowl. Coat well by tossing.
5. Now add your chickpeas to the fryer.
6. Cook for 16 minutes until they turn crispy. Shake them in 4-minute intervals.

Nutrition Info: Calories 133, Carbohydrates 17g, Cholesterol 0mg, Total Fat 5g, Protein 5g, Sugar 0g, Fiber 4g, Sodium 501mg

Potato Tots

Servings: 24
Cooking Time: 35 Minutes
Ingredients:
- 2 peeled sweet potatoes
- Olive oil cooking spray
- ½ teaspoon Cajun seasoning
- Sea salt to taste

Directions:
1. Boil a pot of water. Add the sweet potatoes in it.
2. Keep boiling until you can pierce them using a fork.
3. It should take about 15 minutes. Don't over boil, as they can get too messy for grating. Drain off the liquid. Allow it to cool.
4. Grate the potatoes in a bowl.
5. Now mix your Cajun seasoning carefully.
6. Create tot-shaped cylinders with this mixture.
7. Spray some olive oil on your fryer basket.
8. Keep the tots in it. They should be in 1 row and shouldn't be touching each other or the basket's sides.
9. Apply some olive oil spray on the tots.
10. Heat your air fryer to 200 degrees C or 400 degrees F.
11. Cook for 8 minutes.
12. Flip over and cook for 8 more minutes after applying the olive oil spray again.

Nutrition Info: Calories 22, Carbohydrates 5g, Cholesterol 0mg, Total Fat 0g, Protein 0.4g, Sugar 1g, Fiber 0.7g, Sodium 36mg

Roasted Vegetables

Servings: 4
Cooking Time: 20 Minutes
Ingredients:
- 1 yellow squash, cut into small pieces
- 1 red bell pepper, seeded and cut into small pieces
- ¼ oz. mushrooms, cleaned and halved
- 1 tablespoon of extra-virgin olive oil
- 1 zucchini, cut into small pieces

Directions:
1. Preheat your air fryer. Keep the squash, red bell pepper, and mushrooms in a bowl.
2. Add the black pepper, salt, and olive oil. Combine well by tossing.
3. Keep the vegetables in your fryer basket.
4. Air fry them for 15 minutes. They should get roasted. Stir about halfway into the roasting time.

Nutrition Info: Calories 89, Carbohydrates 8g, Cholesterol 0mg, Total Fat 5g, Protein 3g, Sugar 4g, Fiber 2.3g, Sodium 48mg

Air Fryer Pumpkin Keto Pancakes

Servings: 2
Cooking Time: 5 Minutes
Ingredients:
- ½ cup pumpkin puree
- 1 teaspoon of vanilla extract
- 2 eggs
- ½ cup peanut butter
- ½ teaspoon baking soda

Directions:
1. Use parchment paper to line the basket of your air fryer.
2. Apply some cooking spray.
3. Bring together the eggs, peanut butter, pumpkin puree, baking soda, salt, and eggs in a bowl. Combine well by stirring.
4. Place 3 tablespoons of the batter in each pancake. There should be a half-inch space between them.
5. Keep the basket in your air fryer oven.
6. Cook for 4 minutes at 150 degrees C or 300 degrees F.

Nutrition Info: Calories 586, Carbohydrates 20g, Cholesterol 186mg, Total Fat 46g, Protein 23g, Sugar 9g, Fiber 6g, Sodium 906mg

Buttered Veggies

Servings: 3
Cooking Time: 20 Minutes
Ingredients:
- 1 cup potatoes, chopped
- 1 cup beets, peeled and chopped
- 1 cup carrots, peeled and chopped
- 2 garlic cloves, minced
- Salt and ground black pepper, as required
- 3 tablespoons olive oil

Directions:
1. In a bowl, place all ingredients and toss to coat well.
2. Place the tofu mixture in the greased "Sheet Pan".
3. Press "Power Button" of Ninja Foodi Digital Air Fry Oven and turn the dial to select the "Air Bake" mode.
4. Press the Time button and again turn the dial to set the cooking time to 20 minutes.
5. Now push the Temp button and rotate the dial to set the temperature at 450 degrees F.
6. Press "Start/Pause" button to start.
7. When the unit beeps to show that it is preheated, open the lid.
8. Insert the "Sheet Pan" in oven.
9. Toss the veggie mixture once halfway through.
10. Serve hot.

Nutrition Info: Calories 197 Total Fat 14.2 g Saturated Fat 2 g Cholesterol 0 mg Sodium 123 mg Total Carbs 17.8 g Fiber 3.3 g Sugar 6.9 g Protein 2.2 g

Sweet Potato Hash

Servings: 6
Cooking Time: 15 Minutes
Ingredients:
- 2 sweet potatoes, cubed into small pieces
- 2 tablespoons of olive oil
- 1 teaspoon black pepper, ground
- 1 tablespoon of smoked paprika
- 1 teaspoon dill weed, dried

Directions:
1. Preheat your air fryer to 200 degrees C or 400 degrees F.
2. Toss the olive oil, sweet potatoes, paprika, pepper, and salt in a bowl.
3. Keep this mixture in your air fryer.
4. Now cook for 12 minutes.
5. Check first, and then stir after 8 minutes. Stir after another 2 minutes. It should turn brown and crispy.

Nutrition Info: Calories 203, Carbohydrates 31g, Cholesterol 3mg, Total Fat 7g, Protein 4g, Sugar 6g, Fiber 5g, Sodium 447mg

Roasted Okra

Servings: 1
Cooking Time: 15 Minutes
Ingredients:
- ½ oz. okra, trimmed ends and sliced pods
- ¼ teaspoon salt
- 1 teaspoon olive oil
- 1/8 teaspoon black pepper, ground

Directions:
1. Preheat your air fryer to 175 degrees C or 350 degrees F.
2. Bring together the olive oil, okra, pepper, and salt in a mid-sized bowl.
3. Stir gently.
4. Keep in your air fryer basket. It should be in one single layer.
5. Cook for 5 minutes in the fryer. Toss once and cook for another 5 minutes.
6. Toss once more. Cook again for 2 minutes.

Nutrition Info: Calories 138, Carbohydrates 16g, Cholesterol 0mg, Total Fat 6g, Protein 5g, Sugar 3g, Fiber 7g, Sodium 600mg

Broccoli With Cauliflower

Servings: 6
Cooking Time: 15 Minutes

Ingredients:

- 1-pound broccoli, cut into 1-inch florets
- 1-pound cauliflower, cut into 1-inch florets
- 2 tablespoons butter
- Salt and ground black pepper, as required
- ¼ cup Parmesan cheese, grated

Directions:

1. In a pan of the boiling water, add the broccoli and cook for about 3-4 minutes.
2. Drain the broccoli well.
3. In a bowl, place the broccoli, cauliflower, oil, salt, and black pepper and toss to coat well.
4. Press "Power Button" of Ninja Foodi Digital Air Fry Oven and turn the dial to select the "Air Fry" mode.
5. Press the Time button and again turn the dial to set the cooking time to 15 minutes.
6. Now push the Temp button and rotate the dial to set the temperature at 400 degrees F.
7. Press "Start/Pause" button to start.
8. When the unit beeps to show that it is preheated, open the lid.
9. Arrange the veggie mixture in "Air Fry Basket" and insert in the oven.
10. Toss the veggie mixture once halfway through.
11. Remove from oven and transfer the veggie mixture into a large bowl.
12. Immediately, stir in the cheese and serve immediately.

Nutrition Info: Calories 91 Total Fat 5 g Saturated Fat 2.8 g Cholesterol 13 mg Sodium 131 mg Total Carbs 9 g Fiber 3.9 g Sugar 3.1 g Protein 5 g

Spicy Potato

Servings: 4
Cooking Time: 25 Minutes
Ingredients:
- 2 cups water
- 6 russet potatoes, peeled and cubed
- ½ tablespoon extra-virgin olive oil
- ½ of onion, chopped
- 1 tablespoon fresh rosemary, chopped
- 1 garlic clove, minced
- 1 jalapeño pepper, chopped
- ½ teaspoon garam masala powder
- ¼ teaspoon ground cumin
- ¼ teaspoon red chili powder
- Salt and ground black pepper, as required

Directions:
1. In a large bowl, add the water and potatoes and set aside for about 30 minutes.
2. Drain well and pat dry with the paper towels.
3. In a bowl, add the potatoes and oil and toss to coat well.
4. Press "Power Button" of Ninja Foodi Digital Air Fry Oven and turn the dial to select the "Air Fry" mode.
5. Press the Time button and again turn the dial to set the cooking time to 5 minutes.
6. Now push the Temp button and rotate the dial to set the temperature at 330 degrees F.
7. Press "Start/Pause" button to start.
8. When the unit beeps to show that it is preheated, open the lid.
9. Arrange the potato cubes in "Air Fry Basket" and insert in the oven.
10. Remove from oven and transfer the potatoes into a bowl.
11. Add the remaining ingredients and toss to coat well.
12. Press "Power Button" of Ninja Foodi Digital Air Fry Oven and turn the dial to select the "Air Fry" mode.
13. Press the Time button and again turn the dial to set the cooking time to 20 minutes.
14. Now push the Temp button and rotate the dial to set the temperature at 390 degrees F.
15. Press "Start/Pause" button to start.
16. When the unit beeps to show that it is preheated, open the lid.
17. Arrange the potato mixture in "Air Fry Basket" and insert in the oven.
18. Serve hot.

Nutrition Info: Calories 274 Total Fat 2.3 g Saturated Fat 0.4 g Cholesterol 0 mg Sodium 65mg Total Carbs 52.6 g Fiber 8.5 g Sugar 4.4 g Protein 5.7 g

Corn Nuts

Servings: 8
Cooking Time: 25 Minutes
Ingredients:
- 1 oz. white corn
- 1-1/2 teaspoons salt
- 3 tablespoons of vegetable oil

Directions:
1. Keep the corn in a bowl. Cover this with water. Keep aside for 8 hours minimum for hydration.
2. Drain the corn. Spread it on a baking sheet. They should be in an even layer.
3. Use paper towels to pat dry. Also air dry for 15 minutes.
4. Preheat your air fryer to 200 degrees C or 400 degrees F.
5. Transfer the corn to a bowl. Add salt and oil. Stir to coat evenly.
6. Keep the corn in your air fryer basket in an even layer.
7. Cook for 8 minutes.
8. Shake the basket and cook for 8 minutes more.
9. Shake the basket once more. Cook for 5 more minutes.
10. Transfer to a plate lined with a paper towel.
11. Set aside for allowing the corn nuts to cool. They should be crisp.

Nutrition Info: Calories 240, Carbohydrates 36g, Cholesterol 0mg, Total Fat 8g, Protein 6g, Sugar 1g, Fiber 7g, Sodium 438mg

Veggie Ratatouille

Servings: 4
Cooking Time: 15 Minutes
Ingredients:

- 1 green bell pepper, seeded and chopped
- 1 yellow bell pepper, seeded and chopped
- 1 eggplant, chopped
- 1 zucchini, chopped
- 3 tomatoes, chopped
- 2 small onions, chopped
- 2 garlic cloves, minced
- 2 tablespoons Herbs de Provence
- 1 tablespoon olive oil
- 1 tablespoon balsamic vinegar
- Salt and freshly ground black pepper, to taste

Directions:

1. In a large bowl, add the vegetables, garlic, Herbs de Provence, oil, vinegar, salt, and black pepper and toss to coat well.
2. Transfer vegetable mixture into a greased baking pan.
3. Press "Power Button" of Ninja Foodi Digital Air Fry Oven and turn the dial to select "Air Fry" mode.
4. Press "Time Button" and again turn the dial to set the cooking time to 15 minutes.
5. Now push "Temp Button" and rotate the dial to set the temperature at 355 degrees F.
6. Press "Start/Pause" button to start.
7. When the unit beeps to show that it is preheated, open the lid.
8. Arrange the pan over the wire rack and insert in the oven.
9. When cooking time is complete, open the lid and place the pan aside for about 5 minutes before serving.
10. Serving Suggestions: Serve ratatouille over a cooked grain, such as rice, quinoa, or pasta.
11. Variation Tip: Make sure to use fresh veggies.

Nutrition Info: Calories: 119 Fat: 4.2g Sat Fat: 0.6g Carbohydrates: 20.3g Fiber: 7.3g Sugar: 11.2g Protein: 3.6g

Veggie Kabobs

Servings: 6
Cooking Time: 10 Minutes

Ingredients:

- ¼ cup carrots, peeled and chopped
- ¼ cup French beans
- ½ cup green peas
- 1 teaspoon ginger
- 3 garlic cloves, peeled
- 3 green chilies
- ¼ cup fresh mint leaves
- ½ cup cottage cheese
- 2 medium boiled potatoes, mashed
- ½ teaspoon five-spice powder
- Salt, to taste
- 2 tablespoons corn flour
- Olive oil cooking spray

Directions:

1. In a food processor, add the carrot, beans, peas, ginger, garlic, mint, cheese and pulse until smooth.
2. Transfer the mixture into a bowl.
3. Add the mashed potatoes, five-spice powder, salt and corn flour and with your hands mix until well combined.
4. Shape the mixture into equal-sized small balls.
5. Press each ball around a skewer in a sausage shape.
6. Spray the skewers with cooking spray.
7. Press "Power Button" of Ninja Foodi Digital Air Fry Oven and turn the dial to select "Air Fry" mode.
8. Press "Time Button" and again turn the dial to set the cooking time to 10 minutes.
9. Now push "Temp Button" and rotate the dial to set the temperature at 390 degrees F.
10. Press "Start/Pause" button to start.
11. When the unit beeps to show that it is preheated, open the lid and grease the air fry basket.
12. Arrange the skewers into the prepared air fry basket and insert in the oven.
13. When cooking time is complete, open the lid and transfer the skewers onto a platter.
14. Serve warm.
15. Serving Suggestions: Enjoy these kabobs wt yogurt dip.
16. Variation Tip: You can add spices of your choice in these veggie kabobs

Nutrition Info: Calories: 120, Fat: 0.8g Sat Fat: 0.3g, Carbohydrates: 21.9g Fiber: 4.9g Sugar: 1.8g Protein: 6.3g

Glazed Mushrooms

Servings: 4
Cooking Time: 15 Minutes

Ingredients:

- ¼ cup soy sauce
- ¼ cup honey
- ¼ cup balsamic vinegar
- 2 garlic cloves, chopped finely
- ½ teaspoon red pepper flakes, crushed
- 18 ounces fresh Cremini mushrooms, halved

Directions:

1. In a bowl, place the soy sauce, honey, vinegar, garlic and red pepper flakes and mix well. Set aside.
2. Place the mushroom into the greased baking pan in a single layer.
3. Press "Power Button" of Ninja Foodi Digital Air Fry Oven and turn the dial to select "Air Bake" mode.
4. Press "Time Button" and again turn the dial to set the cooking time to 15 minutes.
5. Now push "Temp Button" and rotate the dial to set the temperature at 350 degrees F.
6. Press "Start/Pause" button to start.
7. When the unit beeps to show that it is preheated, open the lid.
8. Insert the baking pan in oven.
9. After 8 minutes of cooking, place the honey mixture in baking pan and toss to coat well.
10. When cooking time is complete, open the lid and transfer the mushrooms onto serving plates.
11. Serve hot.
12. Serving Suggestions: Topping of fresh chives or marjoram gives a delish touch to mushrooms.
13. Variation Tip: Maple syrup will be an excellent substitute for honey.

Nutrition Info: Calories: 113 Fat: 0.2g Sat Fat: 0g Carbohydrates: 24.7g Fiber: 1g Sugar: 20g Protein: 4.4g

Sweet & Tangy Mushrooms

Servings: 4
Cooking Time: 15 Minutes

Ingredients:

- ¼ cup soy sauce
- ¼ cup honey
- ¼ cup balsamic vinegar
- 2 garlic cloves, chopped finely
- ½ teaspoon red pepper flakes, crushed
- 18 ounces cremini mushrooms, halved

Directions:

1. In a bowl, place the soy sauce, honey, vinegar, garlic and red pepper flakes and mix well. Set aside.
2. Place the mushroom into the greased baking pan in a single layer.
3. Press "Power Button" of Ninja Foodi Digital Air Fry Oven and turn the dial to select the "Air Bake" mode.
4. Press the Time button and again turn the dial to set the cooking time to 15 minutes.
5. Now push the Temp button and rotate the dial to set the temperature at 350 degrees F.
6. Press "Start/Pause" button to start.
7. When the unit beeps to show that it is preheated, open the lid.
8. Insert the baking pan in oven.
9. After 8 minutes of cooking, place the honey mixture in baking pan and toss to coat well.
10. Serve hot.

Nutrition Info: Calories 113 Total Fat 0.2 g Saturated Fat 0 g Cholesterol 0 mg Sodium 9.8 mg Total Carbs 24.7 g Fiber 1 g Sugar 20 g Protein 4.4 g

Spicy Green Beans

Servings: 4
Cooking Time: 25 Minutes

Ingredients:

- ¾ oz. green beans, trimmed
- 1 teaspoon of soy sauce
- 1 tablespoon sesame oil
- 1 garlic clove, minced
- 1 teaspoon of rice wine vinegar

Directions:

1. Preheat your air fryer to 200 degrees C or 400 degrees F.
2. Keep the green beans in a bowl.
3. Whisk together the soy sauce, sesame oil, garlic, and rice wine vinegar in another bowl.
4. Pour the green beans into it.
5. Coat well by tossing. Leave it for 5 minutes to marinate.
6. Transfer half of the beans to your air fryer basket.
7. Cook for 12 minutes. Shake the basket after 6 minutes.
8. Repeat with the other portion of green beans.

Nutrition Info: Calories 81, Carbohydrates 7g, Cholesterol 0mg, Total Fat 5g, Protein 2g, Sugar 1g, Fiber 3g, Sodium 80mg

SNACK & DESSERT RECIPES

Banana Cake

Servings: 4
Cooking Time: 30 Minutes
Ingredients:
- 1 mashed banana
- 1 egg
- 1/3 cup brown sugar
- 3-1/2 tablespoons of butter, room temperature
- 1 cup flour
- 2 tablespoons of honey

Directions:
1. Preheat your air fryer to 160 degrees C or 320 degrees F.
2. Apply cooking spray on a small tube pan.
3. Beat the butter and sugar together in your bowl. It should turn creamy.
4. Bring together the egg, banana, and honey in another bowl.
5. Now whisk this banana mix into your butter mixture. It should be smooth.
6. Stir in the salt and flour into this mixture.
7. Mix the batter until it gets smooth.
8. Keep in the pan and transfer to the air fryer basket.
9. Bake until you see a toothpick coming out clean from the cake.

Nutrition Info: Calories 419, Carbohydrates 57g, Cholesterol 73mg, Total Fat 19g, Protein 5g, Sugar 30g, Fiber 2g, Sodium 531mg

Scotch Eggs

Servings: 6
Cooking Time: 15 Minutes
Ingredients:
- 2 eggs, beaten lightly
- 6 hard-boiled and shelled eggs
- 3 tablespoons of Greek yogurt
- 1/8 teaspoon curry powder
- 1 tablespoon mayonnaise
- 1 cup bread crumbs
- 1 oz. pork sausage
- 1/3 cup flour

Directions:
1. Combine the mayonnaise, yogurt, curry powder, pepper, and salt in a bowl.
2. Keep it refrigerated until you can use it.
3. Platen the 6 pork sausage portions into thin patties.
4. Place an egg at the center of each patty. Wrap sausage around these eggs. Seal all the sides.
5. Preheat your air fryer to 200 degrees C or 390 degrees F.
6. Take flour in a bowl. Beat the eggs into a second bowl.
7. Keep bread crumbs on a plate.
8. Now dip the egg wrapped sausage into flour and then into the beaten egg. Allow the excess portions to drip off.
9. Roll the bread crumbs in. Place on a plate.
10. Apply cooking spray on your fryer basket. Keep the eggs into it. Remember, you shouldn't be overcrowding.
11. Cook for 10 minutes. Turn the eggs after 5 minutes.

Nutrition Info: Calories 501, Carbohydrates 21g, Cholesterol 284mg, Total Fat 37g, Protein 21g, Sugar 3g, Fiber 0.4g, Sodium 945mg

Beef Taquitos

Servings: 6
Cooking Time: 8 Minutes

Ingredients:

- 6 corn tortillas
- 2 cups cooked beef, shredded
- ½ cup onion, chopped
- 1 cup pepper jack cheese, shredded
- Olive oil cooking spray

Directions:

1. Arrange the tortillas onto a smooth surface.
2. Place the shredded meat over one corner of each tortilla, followed by onion and cheese.
3. Roll each tortilla to secure the filling and secure with toothpicks.
4. Spray each taquito with cooking spray evenly.
5. Arrange the taquitos onto the greased "Sheet Pan".
6. Place the tofu mixture in the greased "Sheet Pan".
7. Press "Power Button" of Ninja Foodi Digital Air Fry Oven and turn the dial to select the "Air Fry" mode.
8. Press the Time button and again turn the dial to set the cooking time to 8 minutes.
9. Now push the Temp button and rotate the dial to set the temperature at 400 degrees F.
10. Press "Start/Pause" button to start.
11. When the unit beeps to show that it is preheated, open the lid.
12. Insert the "Sheet Pan" in oven.
13. Serve warm.

Nutrition Info: Calories 228 Total Fat 9.6 g Saturated Fat 4.8 g Cholesterol 67 mg Sodium 235 mg Total Carbs 12.3 g Fiber 1.7 g Sugar 0.6 g Protein 22.7 g

Apple Pies

Servings: 4
Cooking Time: 15 Minutes

Ingredients:

- 2 medium apples, diced
- 6 tablespoons brown sugar
- 1 teaspoon of cornstarch
- 4 tablespoons butter
- ½ tablespoon of grapeseed oil
- 1 teaspoon milk

Directions:

1. Combine butter, apples, and brown sugar in your non-stick skillet.
2. Cook on medium heat for 5 minutes. The apples should get soft.
3. Now dissolve the cornstarch in some cold water.
4. Stir the apple mixture in. Cook until you see the sauce thickening.
5. Take out the apple pie filling. Keep aside for cooling.
6. Unroll your pie crust on a floured surface. Roll out a bit to make the dough surface smooth.
7. Cut your dough into small rectangles. 2 of them should fit into the air fryer.
8. Repeat the process until there are 8 rectangles that are equal.
9. Use water to wet the outer edges of your 4 rectangles.
10. Keep the apple filling at the center. It should be half an inch away from the edges.
11. Roll out your other rectangles. They should be a bit bigger than the ones you have filled up.
12. Keep these rectangles at the top of your filling.
13. Use a fork to crimp the edges for sealing.
14. Now create four small slits at the top portion of your pies.
15. Apply some cooking spray in the air fryer basket.
16. Brush grapeseed oil on the top portion of 2 pies. Keep them in the fryer basket.
17. Bake for 6 minutes. They should become golden brown.
18. Take them out. Repeat with the other 2 pies.
19. Drizzle some milk on the warm pies. Let them dry before serving.

Nutrition Info: Calories 612, Carbohydrates 60g, Cholesterol 31mg, Total Fat 40g, Protein 3g, Sugar 36g, Fiber 3g, Sodium 328mg

Air Fryer Oreos

Servings: 9
Cooking Time: 10 Minutes

Ingredients:

- ½ cup pancake mix
- 9 chocolate sandwich cookies like Oreo®
- 1/3 cup water
- 1 tablespoon of confectioners' sugar

Directions:

1. Mix water and the pancake mix. Combine well.
2. Use parchment paper to line the basket of your air fryer.
3. Apply some cooking spray.
4. Now dip the cookies into your pancake mix. Keep in the fryer basket.
5. They should not touch each other.
6. Preheat your air fryer to 200 degrees C or 400 degrees F.
7. Cook for 4 minutes.
8. Flip over. Cook for 3 more minutes until they turn golden brown.
9. Sprinkle some confectioners' sugar.

Nutrition Info: Calories 78, Carbohydrates 14g, Cholesterol 0mg, Total Fat 2g, Protein 1g, Sugar 5g, Fiber 0.3g, Sodium 156mg

Glazed Figs

Servings: 4
Cooking Time: 10 Minutes
Ingredients:
- 4 fresh figs
- 4 teaspoons honey
- 2/3 cup Mascarpone cheese, softened
- Pinch of ground cinnamon

Directions:
1. Cut each fig into the quarter, leaving just a little at the base to hold the fruit together.
2. Arrange the figs onto a parchment paper-lined sheet pan and drizzle with honey.
3. Place about 2 teaspoons of Mascarpone cheese in the center of each fig and sprinkle with cinnamon.
4. Press "Power Button" of Ninja Foodi Digital Air Fry Oven and turn the dial to select the "Air Broil" mode.
5. Press "Time Button" and again turn the dial to set the cooking time to 10 minutes.
6. Press "Start/Pause" button to start.
7. When the unit beeps to show that it is preheated, open the lid and insert the sheet pan in oven.
8. When cooking time is complete, open the lid and transfer the figs onto a platter.
9. Serve warm.
10. Serving Suggestions: Topping of chopped nuts will add a nice nutty texture.
11. Variation Tip: Select figs that are clean and dry, with smooth, unbroken skin.

Nutrition Info: Calories: 141 Fat: 5.5g Sat Fat: 3.5g Carbohydrates: 19.2g Fiber: 1.9g Sugar: 15g Protein: 5.3g

Banana Split

Servings: 8
Cooking Time: 14 Minutes

Ingredients:
- 3 tablespoons coconut oil
- 1 cup panko breadcrumbs
- ½ cup corn flour
- 2 eggs
- 4 bananas, peeled and halved lengthwise
- 3 tablespoons sugar
- ¼ teaspoon ground cinnamon
- 2 tablespoons walnuts, chopped

Directions:
1. In a medium skillet, melt the coconut oil over medium heat and cook breadcrumbs for about 3-4 minutes or until golden browned and crumbled, stirring continuously.
2. Transfer the breadcrumbs into a shallow bowl and set aside to cool.
3. In a second bowl, place the corn flour.
4. In a third bowl, whisk the eggs.
5. Coat the banana slices with flour and then, dip into eggs and finally, coat with the breadcrumbs evenly.
6. In a small bowl, mix together the sugar and cinnamon.
7. Press "Power Button" of Ninja Foodi Digital Air Fry Oven and turn the dial to select "Air Fry" mode.
8. Press "Time Button" and again turn the dial to set the cooking time to 10 minutes.
9. Now push "Temp Button" and rotate the dial to set the temperature at 280 degrees F.
10. Press "Start/Pause" button to start.
11. When the unit beeps to show that it is preheated, open the lid.
12. Arrange the banana slices into the air fry basket and sprinkle with cinnamon sugar.
13. Insert the basket in the oven.
14. When cooking time is complete, open the lid and transfer the banana slices onto plates to cool slightly
15. Sprinkle with chopped walnuts and serve.
16. Serving Suggestions: Serve with a scoop of strawberry ice cream.
17. Variation Tip: Pecans will be an excellent substitute for walnuts.

Nutrition Info: Calories: 216 Fat: 8.8g Sat Fat: 5.3g Carbohydrates: 26g Fiber: 2.3g Sugar: 11.9g Protein: 3.4g

Chocolate Cake

Servings: 4
Cooking Time: 15 Minutes

Ingredients:
- 3-1/2 tablespoons of butter, softened
- ¼ cup white sugar
- 1 tablespoon of apricot jam
- 1 egg
- 1 tablespoon cocoa powder, unsweetened
- 6 tablespoons of all-purpose flour

Directions:
1. Preheat your air fryer to 160 degrees C or 320 degrees F.
2. Apply cooking spray on a small tube pan.
3. Use an electric mixer to beat the butter and sugar together in your bowl. It should get creamy and light.
4. Add the jam and egg. Combine well by mixing.
5. Now sift in the cocoa powder, flour, and salt. Make sure to mix well.
6. Pour the batter into your pan. Take a spoon and with its backside, level the batter surface.
7. Transfer pan to your air fryer basket.
8. Cook for 10 minutes. A toothpick should come out clean from the cake's center.

Nutrition Info: Calories 283, Carbohydrates 25g, Cholesterol 73mg, Total Fat 19g, Protein 3g, Sugar 15g, Fiber 2g, Sodium 130mg

Cheddar Biscuits

Servings: 8
Cooking Time: 10 Minutes
Ingredients:
- 1/3 cup unbleached all-purpose flour
- 1/8 teaspoon cayenne pepper
- 1/8 teaspoon smoked paprika
- Pinch of garlic powder
- Salt and freshly ground black pepper, to taste
- ½ cup sharp cheddar cheese, shredded
- 2 tablespoons butter, softened
- Nonstick cooking spray

Directions:
1. In a food processor, add the flour, spices, salt and black pepper and pulse until well combined.
2. Add the cheese and butter and pulse until a smooth dough forms.
3. Place the dough onto a lightly floured surface.
4. Make 16 small equal-sized balls from the dough and press each slightly.
5. Press "Power Button" of Ninja Foodi Digital Air Fry Oven and turn the dial to select "Air Bake" mode.
6. Press "Time Button" and again turn the dial to set the cooking time to 10 minutes.
7. Now push "Temp Button" and rotate the dial to set the temperature at 330 degrees F.
8. Press "Start/Pause" button to start.
9. When the unit beeps to show that it is preheated, open the lid and grease the air fry basket.
10. Arrange the biscuits into the prepared air fry basket and insert in the oven.
11. When cooking time is complete, open the lid and place the basket onto a wire rack for about 10 minutes.
12. Carefully invert the biscuits onto the wire rack to cool completely before serving.
13. Serving Suggestions: Serve these cheddar biscuits with the drizzling of garlic butter.
14. Variation Tip: For flaky layers, use cold butter.
Nutrition Info: Calories: 73 Fat: 5.3g Sat Fat: 3.3g Carbohydrates: 4.1g Fiber: 0.2g Sugar: 0.1g Protein: 2.3g

Easy Apple Pies

Servings: 10
Cooking Time: 15 Minutes

Ingredients:

- 2 pie crusts
- 1 can apple pie filling
- 2 tablespoons of cinnamon sugar
- 1 egg, beaten

Directions:

1. Keep 1 pie crust on a floured surface.
2. Roll the dough out with your rolling pin.
3. Take a cookie-cutter. Now create 10 circles by cutting your pie crust.
4. Do this with the 2nd pie crust as well. You should have 20 circles.
5. Fill up half of each circle with the apple pie filling.
6. Keep the second circle on top, creating a mini pie. Make sure not to overfill.
7. Press down edges of your mini peas. Seal.
8. Brush beaten egg on the tops. Sprinkle some cinnamon sugar.
9. Preheat your air fryer to 175 degrees C or 360 degrees F.
10. Apply cooking spray on the fryer basket lightly.
11. Keep your mini peas in the basket. There should be space for air circulation.
12. Bake for 7 minutes. They should turn golden brown.

Nutrition Info: Calories 296, Carbohydrates 35g, Cholesterol 16mg, Total Fat 16g, Protein 3g, Sugar 0g, Fiber 2g, Sodium 225mg

Fried Pickles

Servings: 8

Cooking Time: 10 Minutes

Ingredients:

- 2 tablespoons of sriracha sauce
- ½ cup mayonnaise
- 1 egg
- ½ cup all-purpose flour
- 2 tablespoons of milk
- ¼ teaspoon garlic powder
- 1 jar dill pickle chips

Directions:

1. Mix the sriracha sauce and mayonnaise together in a bowl.
2. Refrigerate until you can use it.
3. Heat your air fryer to 200 degrees C or 400 degrees F.
4. Drain the pickles. Use paper towels to dry them.
5. Now mix the milk and egg together in another bowl.
6. Also mix the cornmeal, flour, garlic powder, pepper, and salt in a third bowl.
7. Dip the pickle chips in your egg mix, and then in the flour mix. Coat both sides lightly. Press the mixture into chips lightly.
8. Apply cooking spray in the fryer basket.
9. Keep the chips in the fryer's basket.
10. Cook for 4 minutes. Flip over and cook for another 4 minutes.
11. Serve with the sriracha mayo.

Nutrition Info: Calories 198, Carbohydrates 15g, Cholesterol 26mg, Total Fat 14g, Protein 3g, Sugar 1g, Fiber 2g, Sodium 1024mg

Air-fried Butter Cake

Servings: 4
Cooking Time: 15 Minutes

Ingredients:

- 1 egg
- 7 tablespoons of butter, room temperature
- 1-2/3 cups all-purpose flour
- ½ cup white sugar
- 6 tablespoons of milk

Directions:

1. Preheat your air fryer to 180 degrees C or 350 degrees F.
2. Apply cooking spray on a small tube pan.
3. Beat ¼ cup and 2 tablespoons of butter. It should be creamy and light.
4. Include the egg. Mix until it gets fluffy and smooth.
5. Stir in the salt and flour now.
6. Add milk. Mix the batter thoroughly.
7. Transfer the batter to your pan. Level the surface with a spoon's back.
8. Keep this pan in the basket of your air fryer.
9. Bake until you see a toothpick coming out clean when inserted.
10. Take out the cake. Set aside for cooling for 5 minutes.

Nutrition Info: Calories 596, Carbohydrates 60g, Cholesterol 102mg, Total Fat 36g, Protein 8g, Sugar 20g, Fiber 1.4g, Sodium 210mg

Air Fryer Beignets

Servings: 7
Cooking Time: 15 Minutes

Ingredients:

- ½ cup all-purpose flour
- 1 egg, separated
- ½ teaspoon of baking powder
- 1-1/2 teaspoons melted butter
- ¼ cup white sugar
- ½ teaspoon of vanilla extract

Directions:

1. Preheat your air fryer to 185 degrees C or 370 degrees F.
2. Whisk together the sugar, flour, butter, egg yolk, vanilla extract, baking powder, salt, and water in a bowl. Combine well by stirring.
3. Use an electric hand mixer to beat the white portion of the egg in a bowl.
4. Fold this into the batter.
5. Now use a small ice cream scoop to add the mold.
6. Keep the mold into the air fryer basket.
7. Fry for 10 minutes in your air fryer.
8. Take out the mold and the pop beignets carefully.
9. Flip them over on a round of parchment paper.
10. Now transfer the parchment round with the beignets into the fryer basket.
11. Cook for 4 more minutes.

Nutrition Info: Calories 99, Carbohydrates 16g, Cholesterol 29mg, Total Fat 3g, Protein 2g, Sugar 9g, Fiber 0.2g, Sodium 74mg

Red Velvet Cupcakes

Servings: 12
Cooking Time: 12 Minutes

Ingredients:

- For Cupcakes:
- 2 cups refined flour
- ¾ cup icing sugar
- 2 teaspoons beet powder
- 1 teaspoon cocoa powder
- ¾ cup peanut butter
- 3 eggs
- For Frosting:
- 1 cup butter
- 1 (8-ounce) package cream cheese, softened
- 2 teaspoons vanilla extract
- ¼ teaspoon salt
- 4½ cups powdered sugar
- For Garnishing:
- ½ cup fresh raspberries

Directions:

1. For cupcakes: in a bowl, add all the ingredients and with an electric whisker, whisk until well combined.
2. Place the mixture into silicone cups.
3. Press "Power Button" of Ninja Foodi Digital Air Fry Oven and turn the dial to select "Air Fry" mode.
4. Press "Time Button" and again turn the dial to set the cooking time to 12 minutes.
5. Now push "Temp Button" and rotate the dial to set the temperature at 340 degrees F.
6. Press "Start/Pause" button to start.
7. When the unit beeps to show that it is preheated, open the lid.
8. Arrange the silicone cups into the air fry basket and insert in the oven.
9. When cooking time is complete, open the lid and place the silicone cups onto a wire rack to cool for about 10 minutes.
10. Carefully invert the cupcakes onto the wire rack to completely cool before frosting.
11. For frosting: in a large bowl, mix well butter, cream cheese, vanilla extract, and salt.
12. Add the powdered sugar, one cup at a time, whisking well after each addition.
13. Spread frosting over each cupcake.
14. Garnish with raspberries and serve.
15. Serving Suggestions: Garnishing of sprinkles will add a festive touch in cupcakes.
16. Variation Tip: Measure the ingredients with care.

Nutrition Info: Calories: 599, Fat: 31.5g, Sat Fat: 16g Carbohydrates: 73.2g, Fiber: 2g Sugar: 53.4g, Protein: 9.3g

Basic Hot Dogs

Servings: 4
Cooking Time: 5 Minutes
Ingredients:
- 4 hot dogs
- 4 hot dog buns

Directions:
1. Preheat your air fryer to 200 degrees C or 390 degrees F.
2. Keep the buns in your fryer basket. Cook for 2-3 minutes.
3. Transfer them to a plate.
4. Keep your hot dogs in the air fryer basket. Cook for 3 minutes.
5. Place them in the buns.

Nutrition Info: Calories 317, Carbohydrates 23g, Cholesterol 24mg, Total Fat 21g, Protein 9g, Sugar 4g, Fiber 1g, Sodium 719mg